The Forgotten Faithful

The

Forgotten Faithful

The Christians of the Holy Land

Said Aburish

QUARTET BOOKS

First published in Great Britain by Quartet Books Limited 1993
A member of the Namara Group
27/29 Goodge Street, London W1P 1FD

British Library Cataloguing in Publication Data
Aburish, Said K.
    Forgotten Faithful: Christians of the
    Holy Land
    I. Title
    209.5694

    ISBN 0 7043 7036 0

Typeset by Contour Typesetters, Southall, London
Printed and bound in Great Britain by
BPCC Hazells Ltd.
Member of BPCC Ltd.

ACKNOWLEDGEMENTS

Researching and writing this book depended on the generous help of many people outside and inside the occupied territories. My thanks to all of them, particularly Afif Safia, Jonathan Khuttab, Doris Salah, Naim Ateeq, Camille Nassar, Albert Aggezarian, Jeanne Khattan, Jad Izhaq, Anton Sansour, Father Peter Dubrell SJ, Rami Meo, Chris McConville, David Newhouse, Othman Halaq, Yehuda Litani, Bernard Sabella, Aziz Shehadeh, Roula Amin and all the other people who consented to be interviewed. Very special thanks are due Diana Safia who neglected her own work to provide me with names, lists and telephone numbers and to set up appointments and provide me with general guidance.

Lastly, undertaking this writing project wouldn't have been possible without an unencumbered generous grant from the Authors' Foundation/K. Blundell Trust. My thanks, and hopefully the readers', go to the trustees of these organizations.

CONTENTS

The Seat of Pilate   1

Life Under the Occupation
Bullets and Stones Don't Discriminate   19
A Licence to Visit Mr Jesus   31
A Village Called Abboud   46
The Prospect of a Haunted House   61

A House Divided
Islam Inflamed   77
The Christians Against Themselves   96

Christian Voices, Christian Fears
A Glimmer of Hope   117
The Triumph of Christian Optimism   129
The Politican – Hanan Ashrawi   141

An Uncertain Future   152

The Forgotten Faithful

THE SEAT OF PILATE

The four Israeli soldiers walking along east Jerusalem's Salaheddine Street on guard duty with their rifles at the ready reacted to the strident call to Muslim prayer by exchanging comments of derision and then broke into challenging irreverent laughter. It was 5.00 p.m. on 2 September 1991, and the Muslim claim to Jerusalem which resounds from the loudspeakers of the city's minarets five times a day was confronting the harsh reality of the Israeli claim. A mere fifty yards away, St George's Anglican Cathedral looked hauntingly forsaken, enveloped in an eerie silence which bespoke the plight of the Christians of the Holy Land. It was as if St George's and all the other Christian churches and shrines within view, together with the Christianity they represented, were overshadowed by the shrillness of the Muslim claim and the armed Israeli counter-claim. It was a strong reflection of the reduced Christian presence and status.

The incident along Salaheddine Street is but a small manifestation of the disputed Israeli and Muslim Jerusalem which is the subject of unhappy reporting whenever the press examines the prospects for a settlement of the Arab-Israeli problem. There is the indivisible Jewish Jerusalem, the city of peace, the site of the third temple and the capital of Israel and supreme symbol of its redemption; and there is the

Muslim Jerusalem, Al-Quds or the holy, the home of the Dome of The Rock whence the Prophet Muhammad ascended to heaven to meet his maker, to the Muslims their unnegotiable third holiest city. The conflict between these two Jerusalems and the hate it generates is so blinding it excludes all else, even the uncompeting idea of a spiritual Christian Jerusalem potentially infectious in its gentility. The outside world's view is determined by the merciless realities of power politics and almost everybody recognizes all or part of the Jewish and Muslim claims but wholly at the expense of a solidly historic Christian one and the welfare of the local Christians.

My friend Diana Safia, a descendant of one of Jerusalem's old Roman Catholic families, encapsulates the feeling of frustration of her overlooked Christian co-religionists with a bitterness which contrasts with her usual sunny outlook on life. 'We have been marginalized; it is if we don't have a claim, worse, as if we don't exist.'

Hard as it is, Diana Safia's refrain understates the fight for survival facing the Christians of Jerusalem and the rest of the occupied territories of the West Bank and Gaza. It isn't only that they're neglected and oppressed, the only response they have available to them, emigration, means their eventual disappearance from the Holy Land.

Twenty-five years of Israeli occupation have been disastrous for Palestinian Christians. In addition to the widely known closures of schools, imprisonment and torture of children, deportation of dissenters and activists, the expropriation of land owned by individuals and church-owned property, the Christians' primary sources of income, tourism and its subsidiary service businesses, have been the targets of special Israeli attempts to control them. In other words, when it comes to the Israeli occupation, the Christians have suffered more than their Muslim countrymen because they have more of what the Israelis want.

Furthermore, the rising tide of Islamic fundamentalism is confronting the Christians with new problems against most of which they cannot protest without endangering the local social balance, indeed their Palestinian identity. Muslim fanatics have raised the Crescent on church towers. Christian cemeteries have been desecrated, the statues of the Virgin Mary have been destroyed and, for the first time ever, the Palestinian Christians are facing constraints on their liberal way of life. In Gaza, a Muslim fundamentalist stronghold, Christian women have to wear headscarves and long sleeves or face stoning, and Christian-owned shops have to close on the Muslim sabbath of Friday instead of on Sunday.

These combined pressures come at a time of strain between the local Christian communities and both their local church leadership and the mainline churches in the West. The mainline churches in the West are accused of not doing enough to help them financially or drawing attention to their plight, for fear of appearing anti-Semitic and to a lesser degree anti-Muslim. The local church leaders are caught between their parishioners' cry for help and the attitude of their mother churches and have been undermined by their identification with the latter. In addition to problems with the mainline churches, Christian evangelist groups from the United States, Holland and other countries support the State of Israel at the expense of local Christians. The evangelists accept the recreation of Israel as the prelude to the second coming to the extent of ignoring local Christian rights and feelings, a fact overlooked by Muslim zealots who blame the local Christians for not curbing their insensitive pro-Israeli co-religionists.

Two subsidiary problems contribute towards closing the ring of helplessness which is choking the local Christian communities of the Holy Land. The suffering inflicted on them by others and the direct and indirect results of the neglect of outside Christianity still haven't induced their local church leaders to cooperate in establishing a common, protective Christian position. The traditional quarrel, alongside other disputes between the Roman Catholic and Greek Orthodox churches, continues and it stands in the way of creating a constructive Christian front. Furthermore, the Israelis make the appearance of favouring them against their Muslim nationals, a divide-and-rule policy which contributes towards inflaming the feelings of ignorant Muslims who do not understand the reasons behind the Israeli actions and use them to justify whatever anti-Christian feeling exists.

The seeming insignificance and subtlety of the Israeli soldiers' action in Salaheddine Street did not diminish its meaning for me. It took place on the first day of my two-month stay in Jerusalem to investigate the plight of the neglected Christians of the occupied territories. I was returning to my hotel after a three-hour walk along the streets and alleys of the Holy City which I had embarked on to reacquaint myself with its unique Christian atmosphere.

The streets, roads, walks, valleys, springs, fields, monasteries, nunneries, hospitals and, above all, tombs carry Christian names and are rich in Christian history. I recalled that, even without counting the evangelists and the born-again Christians, there are 274 Christian churches with a presence in Jerusalem, and one cannot walk for long without seeing a priest or a nun or a person whose dress betrays a religious affiliation. In fact, judged by the abundance of Christian churches, monuments and ruins, the number of Christian organizations and the presence of their representatives, Jerusalem may very well be the most Christian city in the world. The reasons behind the two historical Christian attitudes to the place – St Augustine's expression of enchantment ('shadow of a city') and the violent approach of the crusaders – still obtain.

This was the background against which the muted but significant Jewish-Muslim confrontation took place in front of me, and it reinforced the commitment I had developed during previous trips to speak on behalf of the Christians of Jerusalem and the occupied territories. For though Jerusalem and the Christian claim to it are a natural symbol of the plight of the local Christian community, the problem they face is a much larger one which covers all the Christians in the occupied territories.

The pressures by Israel, the Muslim fundamentalists, the harsh economic conditions, the ineffective, divided church leadership and the lack and unreliability of outside help have led most of the Christians to emigrate. Their numbers are already down to 42,000, a mere three per cent of the total

Arab population of the territories, compared with 130,000 who were there at the start of the Israeli occupation in 1967. The number of Christians in Jerusalem is down to 4,000, in the disturbing words of the outspoken Camille Nassar of the local YMCA, 'It would take four Boeing 747s and Jerusalem would cease to have a Christian presence.' And even the 42,000 who remain have had to accommodate their antagonists, 'to corrupt' their Christianity, in order to survive.

On Sunday 8 September, six days after my arrival and three days after my meeting with Camille Nassar, I made the required visit to the Church of the Holy Sepulchre. I stood in the courtyard and watched groups of tourists go in and out of the place led by gesturing guides. Only a handful of local Christians were there, a few tired-looking old men and women in reverent black. I turned to a teenage boy selling tourist trinkets and asked him about the small number of local people and their composition. His answer which he offered without hesitation was the locally accepted one. 'Most of our young people are gone; they have emigrated. What you see is what is left.'

These are the conditions surrounding the Christian presence, emigration and the subsequent, but one hopes stoppable, crisis of Christian disappearance. While nothing is being done to change or ease the local conditions which have created this sad situation, nobody sees fit to speak on their behalf and the Muslim pressure in particular is gaining strength every day, emigration is being facilitated by the existence of Palestinian Christian communities worldwide and by the policies of host countries (e.g. the United States, Canada and Australia) who find it easier to accept qualified Christians than to help them continue in their homeland. The acceleration in the level of emigration and the ensuing danger to Christian existence have produced a rare united act by religious leaders; it has led the heads of the Catholic, Greek Orthodox and Anglican churches to appeal to the embassies of several countries not to facilitate the disappearance of their remaining faithful. But even if this appeal were to succeed, it would represent no more than a stop-gap measure, a step far short of a permanent solution.

The growing prospect of a Holy Land Christianity reduced to stones, a museum or tourist faith without people, a Jerusalem without believers in Christ, is more serious than that of a Rome without a Pope or a Canterbury without an archbishop. It is tantamount to a criminal act which transcends a single church and strikes a blow at the foundations and the very idea of Christianity.

Tragic as this is, it is important to establish whether the Christians' present problems are new ones or old ones made worse by the present circumstances. The marginalization of the Christians of the Holy Land between the Israeli threat and the Muslim counterthreat, is the third historical challenge to their existence. The first occurred when Byzantium tried to eradicate the Coptic and Armenian presence (then the only local Christians) over issues of doctrine. And the second arose when the Crusaders tried to replace the local Christianity with one beholden to Rome.

The three threats stem from the same root cause, the wish of outsiders to subordinate local Christians to their ways. Byzantium and the Crusaders wanted to change the identity of the local Christians and through that to represent them and speak for them. The local Christians were called upon to place religion ahead of nationality, which in both ancient cases meant adherence to an outside rather than an indigenous church. Both attempts failed; the local churches survived and maintained their local character and nationality.

Now, for over a century, the ascendancy of the West has resurrected the old issue. The Christians of the Holy Land have been under heavy pressure to compromise their nationalism and become agents for the Western churches, advocates and protectors of Western interests. Beyond the Western churches' attempts to place their religious affiliation above the immediate demands of nationalism, is crude interference in local church affairs by nation states. For example, France has tried to adopt the local Roman Catholic church and protect its interests, to reduce it to France's religious presence in the Holy Land. And the British have tried to extend the same type of hegemony over the Greek Orthodox and Anglican churches. Had these combined church and state efforts succeeded they would have distanced the local Christians from their Muslim compatriots. This modern attempt has been rejected, and the Christians have opted for the flag instead of the cross. However, sadly, this has only placed them in a more precarious position. Now the twin threats from Israel and the Muslim fundamentalists have eroded their local base; one wants them out of the way and the other limits their freedom. Islamic fundamentalism is questioning their national identity; at the same time the present danger may be more serious than the past ones, as it leaves them with nothing to fall back on.

This is a huge tragedy because twentieth-century Palestinianism would be considerably poorer without the Christians' presence. Their contributions to their country and the welfare of its people have always been beyond their numbers and they have never suffered from the sectarianism which renders questionable the position of some of their co-religionists in Lebanon.

This contribution may explain the intensity of the Israeli pressure on the Christian community. Certainly the Israelis have an interest in muffling the voice of the Palestinian Christians, a people who help show the world that it is wrong to see the Palestinian problem as a conflict between forward-looking Jews and backward Muslims. This has not stopped the rising intolerance of Islamic fundamentalism and the consequent constraints on the Christians' way of life and questioning of their national commitment, two shameful elements which are confounded by the unquestionable facts of a healthy, constructive Palestinian Christianity.

My friend Stepho Stephan, a Christian Palestinian of deep commitment whose past political activities as a Palestinian nationalist landed him in a Jordanian prison for four years, offers a telling analogy which reveals the essence of the Palestinian Christians' status in their country. 'They resemble the Sunni Muslims of Lebanon. There's a bigness about them and what they do, a grand, almost elegant assumption of responsiblity in all fields. When it comes to the Palestinian problem they occupy a house above ground, they are unique in their contribution.'

Stepho's eloquent words are apt, and compel a more detailed review of the position of the Palestinian Christians in the affairs of their country this century. A statistical abstract doesn't tell the story, what matters is a picture of who and what the Christians are, an appreciation of their contributions in the areas of education, politics and business and as leaders in some professional areas such as law and medicine.

In Jerusalem I begin to look for distinguishing signs of the Christian presence. It is necessary to go beyond the old city with its ancient churches and beautiful old houses and the towns of Ramallah and Bethlehem with their unique Christian-Arab atmosphere and the wholesomeness they manifest. I am looking for the bigness Stepho spoke about.

My Israeli journalist friend Yehuda Litani accepts Stepho's description and expresses amazement at my lack of direction. 'They have been decimated, literally, but I can show you how many of them lived and through that you can tell much about them.' Yehuda eventually takes me on a tour of the Christian quarters of new Jerusalem which were occupied by Israel in 1948.

Our tour takes us through Talbieh, Kattamoun and Bak'a Al-Fouqa and Yehuda patiently points out houses and recites the names of their previous owners. I am dumbfounded by the beauty of the areas and size and elegance of the houses I see. This section of Jerusalem contains excellent examples of Mediterranean architecture built of hard stone, the streets are wide and full of trees and one gets the impression that their planners were ahead of their time. But the over-whelming physical aspect has an attendant Christian spirit. Yehuda shows me the house of the late Khalil Sakakini and proceeds to tell me of his contribution in the field of education, how he built the model Omaria school which still stands beautiful around the corner and of his contributions in other areas of education such as the publishing of up-to-date Arabic language texts used throughout the Middle East. I am dazed by the beautiful buildings I see around Salameh Square, and Yehuda explains how the wealthy Salameh family was involved in dozens of charitable organizations.

There are houses of pioneer surgeons who worked in public hospitals, famous lawyers who took time out to defend the poor, political leaders and businessmen with commercial interests throughout the Middle East and there are impressive clubs and social centres. It still remains the most attractive part of Jerusalem and is where many Israeli politicians live.

By the time we finish our tour, I am totally convinced that the Christians had an exalted position among Palestinians, the attractive combination of a wealthy presence and a very Christian, remarkable sense of social commitment. Yehuda leaves me at my hotel after telling me not to forget that the Christians were 'the face' of Palestine and 'in some ways still are'. This Palestinian Christian assumption of national and nationalistic position showed and continues to show across a spectrum of activities which reflect a total sense of belonging; they do not have and have never had the problems of people who live in a society which for the most part holds alien beliefs. Until recently, this position and the roles individual Christians carved for themselves were never questioned and, except for the top leadership position, nothing was ever denied them or stood in their way.

During the 1930s, '40s, and '50s the Palestinians' chief spokesman in international forums, Emil Ghoury, was a Christian and a firebrand of the old school whom the Mufti of Jerusalem, then leader of the Palestinians, often had a very difficult time controlling. Yet Ghoury, like so many others, was a representative of mainstream Palestinian Christian thinking; their only separateness from their Muslim compatriots was in trying to do more for their country and because their education placed them at the front line. Ghoury's younger brother Raja'i affixed Muhammad to his first name in the traditional Muslim way to denote the absence of any difference between the two religions. As a young man I was once present when Raja'i became extremely annoyed because someone questioned his adopted name. (Christianity in the PLO and elsewhere manifest the same determination; ten years ago my Palestinian journalist friend Jihad Al-Khazen named his son Muhammad for the same reason.)

Any presentation of the Palestinian Christian position must start with George Antonious. His *Arab Awakening*, published in the 1930s, remains as vital today as it was then, and it delineates the political and social tensions of the Arabs' search for identity more clearly and completely than any other work.

George Antonious, a Cambridge graduate who died in 1942, never tired of preaching the Palestinian and Arab causes and for so many years he was their most widely accepted spokesman in the West. After his death the torch was carried by his wife Katy. Though not a writer or historian, she energetically devoted herself to social work and continued George's teachings by opening her house to thousands of foreign visitors, including most journalists, who wanted to hear about the Palestinian side of the Arab-Israeli problem. Katy died ten years ago, but the Christian spirit of the Antonious family marches on in the person of Katy and George's daughter Soraya. An attractive, elegant and exceptionally talented writer who's at home using Arabic, English or French, Soraya has written three novels, presenting a remarkable fictional depiction of the tragedy of Palestine and its people.

The Antoniouses' achievement is exceptional but there are other examples which reflect the attitude the family represents. The American historian Arthur Schlesinger Jr states, 'No American scholar has written more fondly of the Arab quest for identity than the Palestinian-American Edward W. Said of Columbia University, N.Y.' A proud Jerusalemite, Professor Said is often on American radio and television to explain the plight of his people. He is the most eloquent of all the Palestinian spokesmen. Not only has he waged a brave, time-consuming, exhausting and indeed successful battle to educate the American people and others in the intricacies of the Palestinian problem, but everybody agrees that listening to him is 'fun, he turns a complicated problem into a worthwhile listening experience.' Both his sisters Rosemary and Jane are also writers of articles and books about the Palestinian problem.

The contributions of the Antoniouses and the Saids in the

field of scholarship are matched by countless others who are equally effective, though less well known. Dr Anton Sansour, President of Bethlehem University, is a model of the Christian educator operating, successfully, under the present difficult conditions which prevail in the West Bank. Not only does he combine a sharp intellect with an attractive personality rooted in his local background but he also acts as a pathfinder for what is possible and practical in the circumstances. Under him the university has grown until it now accommodates over eight hundred students of all denominations taught by teachers from many different nationalities. The various disciplines are constantly being broadened and, with the utmost deliberateness and delicacy, the quality of the syllabus and instruction is on the rise. The university's graduates occupy positions in all walks of life; the West Bank and Gaza are full of 'Sansour children'. One of them has commented, 'He's a great educator, even his jokes, and he's full of them, teach you something.'

I am in the same Bethlehem University which bears Dr Sansour's stamp to meet with Professors Jeanne Kattan, Mai Nassar and Leila Bshara. They belong to three different Christian sects, but that matters considerably less than the singleness of purpose which binds them. They teach English and other disciplines within the humanities and are full of healthy and strong ideas about their role in society. They criticize their churches' antiquated attitudes and speak passionately of a modern, responsive Christianity; they are full of ideas on how the PLO should conduct itself; they refer to the achievements of some of their students with pride and speak of the future with an optimistic realism which leaves little room for despair. They recall the Palestinian Christian educators I have heard about all my life and I leave them with the satisfaction of having met real Christianity and seen that it works.

The Palestinian Christian scholar–educator has always been one of the strongest links which hold the Palestinians together. Sakakini, Antonious, Said, Sansour, Nassar, Kattan and Bshara are representative of a large group of people who have answered the call to duty. Their teachings and preachings are Christian in the broadest sense of the word – they all are practising believers with a remarkable sense of community, humanists who find satisfaction through action as much as prayer – and they do not discriminate. Today a high percentage of the professors and teachers at Beir Zeit University (by far the largest Palestinian institution of higher education) and most of the occupied territories' private and public schools are Christian and even missionary schools have given up their archaic approaches owing to the influence of local teachers who constantly remind them of the immediate needs of the community. Most of the teachers and educators could easily go to more lucrative jobs in other places but stay where they are to serve their people.

If the Christian contribution in the field of scholarship and education is known only to the interested few, the Christian involvement in Palestinian politics is there for everybody to see. And while it is true that some of the present manifestations of this involvement and the people who represent it are highly questionable, the source of the participants' commitment isn't; they do what they do because they're Palestinian Christians who are expressing their nationalistic feeling towards their country. As a matter of fact their overzealousness can be seen as an attempt to eliminate any doubt regarding whether the flag comes ahead of the cross.

Beside Emily Ghoury, the names of the Palestinian Christian politicians Khalil Bedas, Alfred Roch, Fuad Saba, George Humsi and Hanna Asfour mean little now. They were Ghoury's colleagues, members of political groups which flourished in Palestine early this century. They led the fight for an independent Palestine and resisted all British and Jewish attempts to drive a wedge between them and their Muslim compatriots. There wasn't a single instance when these individuals or the Christian community as a whole didn't participate fully in the struggle towards independence.

During the 1948 Arab-Israeli War, the Christians fought alongside their Muslim brothers. But it was later, after the repeated Arab defeats at the hands of the Israelis, that special brands of Palestinian Christian politics came to the surface. As in other fields, Christian sensitivity responded to the catastrophies more openly and their forefront position drew them towards a radical response.

George Habbash is probably the best known Christian politican to devote himself to radical action. He is the founder chairman of the Popular Front for the Liberation of Palestine, an armed struggle group which has not shied away from violent action against Israel and its supporters. In justifying his advocacy of violence and reconciling it with Christian teachings, Habbash is quite forthright, 'We're resisters; violence has been forced upon us; we've been left without an alternative and our attitude is religiously justified.' Right or wrong – and the Christian churches are divided on Habbash's point and, in personal terms, the way of the gun is not my way – he is a living component of Palestinian politics and remains extremely popular with disaffected groups including many frustrated young people, most of whom are Muslims.

Wadi' Haddad and Naif Hawatmeh are two less well known politicans who adopted violent action as a way of trying to recover Palestinian rights. Wadi' Haddad, like Habbash a medical doctor who became radicalized treating poor Palestinians, is now dead, but he was responsible for some of the more celebrated and condemned raids and highjackings. And Hawatmeh preaches extra radicalism through his Democratic Front for the Liberation of Palestine.

But Christian political involvement doesn't stop with radical politics and the fame or notoriety they produce; there are many others who show their nationalism in gentler ways without diminishing their sense of duty. Nowadays Hanan Ashrawi is the voice of the Palestinians in the international arena and the best known among this group and her achievement is very substantial. Hanna Seniora is another moderate Christian politician committed to a peaceful solution to whom the world listens and among the most energetic of the West Bank's political activists. And within the PLO proper there are many hard-working loyal Christians who excel in their devotion to the cause of their country. Even in the area of Palestinian representation abroad, the Christians are in the forefront. Afif Safia, the

courteous PLO Legate to the United Kingdom, has overcome
the stigma attached to his quasi-official position and, through
sheer hard work, has become one of the most popular
diplomats in London.

After the eloquent Ashrawi the most impressive living
moderate Christian politician is Elias Freij, the mayor of
Bethlehem. Short and rotund with a spring in his step, Freij is
a one-man band. In addition to his mayoral duties, he is
involved in all aspects of local and international politics
including the critical area of contacts with Palestinian
Christians living all over the world. 'My aim is to create a
oneness of purpose and effort,' says Freij. He proceeds to
explain how the divisions dissipate the strength of the
Palestinian national movement and within that the efforts of
the Christians as a group. He tells of a recent trip he took to
the Americas and gives me a copy of his schedule. In three
days in Washington DC Freij managed to see two senators,
five congressmen and gave six newspaper and television
interviews. He met with dozens of Palestinian and Arab
immigrés in Mexico and Chile and urged them to maintain
their links with the people of the occupied territories and
think of ways to help them through their present difficulties,
such as giving them assistance in starting small industries.
While I am with him three press interviews are being
arranged and he makes a date to meet with a member of a
poor Bedouin tribe and another to meet with a fellow
member of the Palestinian delegation to the peace conference. Like many others before him he doesn't question his
role and moves forward in the best traditions of Christian
involvement in the affairs of their country.

After education and politics, and the order of their
positions isn't accidental but a reflection of the importance I
attach to each, comes the role of the Palestinian businessman
public servant. In many ways this is a virtual Christian
monopoly and it is here, because the people involved seek no
glory beyond serving, that the true spirit of the Palestinian
Christians shows itself.

The Sabbaghs, Tammaris, Attallahs, Sanbars and Boulouses
may be contractors, importers, bankers and property people

but they find time to send needy students to universities, sponsor study groups, defend poor people in courts and donate and collect money for Palestinian charities. As with educators and politicians, their Christianity, a mellow variety regardless of the church to which any of them belongs, endows them with a human attitude and their Palestinianism with a proud commitment, and it is this blend which produces an enviable wholesomeness which infects its surroundings and which has made the Palestinians the most educated and organized people in the Middle East. When I broached the subject of this book with him, construction magnate Ramzi Sanbar said, 'Well done, tell the world we've always been there and that we're proud of who and what we are.' Everything I know tells me that Sanbar is right, that the Palestinian Christians used their Christian heritage to revitalize a whole society and that they continue to use their Christianity to rise above the crises confronting them. In fact this has always been so. To realize how important their presence and contribution are, one has only to take the Christian element out of the Palestinian equation and think of how it would emasculate Palestinianism. Little wonder that Israel wants them out of the way and surely this must confirm the level of blindness which envelopes the local Muslim fundamentalist movement.

The following oral history of the Christians of the Holy Land is a collection of stories and statements reflecting the conditions of the Palestinian Christians and the dark tunnel ahead of them. It may sound like an obituary, in the victims' own words. It is certainly a tragic story that should have been told sometime back. But, unfortunately for the Forgotten Faithful, telling their story in this form is unlikely to lead to a serious change in their conditions. All someone like me can do is hope that the land of miracles will give us a new one.

LIFE UNDER THE OCCUPATION

BULLETS AND STONES DON'T
DISCRIMINATE

Perhaps it was destiny, fate or something of the sort, something that we cannot subject to reason or logic as we understand and apply them. That day I certainly did a thing I didn't usually do, and I did it because of some unexplainable inner urge, or an outside influence of an equally mysterious nature.

It is 27 September 1991 and already the hottest September on record, but I still decide to walk the mile and a half to my afternoon appointment at the Convent of the Sisters of St Joseph in Prophets Street. Several taxi drivers, aware of the brutality of the unabating heat at three-thirty in the afternoon, make a point of slowing down to offer me rides. I turn down their offers and continue walking. Other people are more sensible; Prophets Street is empty and much of it is an extremely steep climb towards my destination.

I am walking slowly, dragged down by the heat, and my clothes are sticking to my body; ahead of me are four teenagers in religious school garb – *yarmulka*, black trousers, white shirt – and I am catching up with them; soon I am right behind them. I notice that even for the heat they are walking unusually slowly while making mocking sounds, a cross between the howls of cowboys and the shrieks of children breaking up for the school holidays.

It is right ahead of them, the object of their derision, a triangular black figure in a habit which resembles no other I have ever seen and reaches all the way down to the ground. It is a nun, and judging by the way she is moving and her obvious lack of speed, an old one. The teenagers gesture rudely right behind her and I draw closer, the distance between us now no more than five yards. I can't tell much about her from behind, but I determine she is using a cane of natural wood, I glimpse it, and hear her try to dig it into the ground for support.

I decide to stay behind the school children; I am convinced that their sounds and gestures are leading them into uncharted territory, that they are working themselves into a state which might lead to violence. They know that I am right behind them but they ignore me; my presence seems to have very little effect on their behaviour. Our agonizingly slow three-tiered procession continues for about four blocks, until we reach the top of the climb and Prophets Street becomes level. There is still nobody in sight and I have to act on my own and face the consequences. I convince myself that the plan I have thought of will work.

I move around the boys and place myself between them and the nun and walk behind her, at her pace, without looking back. I know they are a mere yard or so behind me, and I can see them in my mind's eye gesturing rudely, but I don't say anything. I turn to face them, suddenly, without preliminaries; and I discover that I am right.

I am walking backwards and talking to them. 'Listen, you're a very nice bunch of kids and I am sure all of you come from good families, but it isn't nice to gesture rudely behind people's backs and make silly noises. I don't care about me, but she is nothing but an elderly nun. Please leave her alone.'

My comments are met by unfriendly answers in Hebrew, and the youngest among them, who can't be a day over fourteen, makes a farting sound with his mouth and laughs out loud. Their voices are getting high and I decide to forgo my face-to-face confrontation tactic and take a chance by turning my back to them and continuing to place myself between them and the nun.

We are one block from the convent and I have to decide whether to continue to try to protect the nun or to go to my appointment. Unexpectedly, she turns into a small side alley,

Ethiopia Street, and I find myself continuing behind her, though not without knowledge that this is much more dangerous than being in the wider Prophets Street. Another decision is needed and I draw parallel to the nun to discover that she is black and confirm that she is indeed elderly with a deeply wrinkled face full of reverence and pain.

'Sister, do you speak English?'

Her head moves from side to side in answer.

I resort to whispering to avoid having the boys hear me and recognize my national identity. 'How about Arabic, do you speak Arabic?'

Once again her head goes from side to side in denial.

'Well, we're in trouble.'

No sooner are the words out of my mouth than the boys shoot past us and run around the bend in the street so that we can't see them. I draw a deep sigh of relief and look at the sister, preparing to try to ask her where she's going. I am not allowed to finish. The boys have reappeared and they're facing us with stones in their hands and we stop.

The nun uses her cane as a prop and straightens her aged, bent body. She faces the boys and I jump between her and them, but a little too late. A stone hits her on the shoulder and another on the arm. I start shouting. 'For God's sake stop it, stop it, help somebody, HELP, HELP PLEASE.' Stones are flying around us, but my screaming unbalances them and they're missing us. Two men came out of one of the nearby buildings, then a third and they exchange quick words and run after the boys who turn tail the moment they see them.

The nun looks at me as if to check that I am all right and I do the same for her. The Israeli men, our saviours, are back. They apologize to me and try to cross the language barrier with her. Clearly they are extremely embarrassed. Two of the men walk with her to a door only six yards ahead and one is talking to me and I am telling him the story from its beginning and we both stop to watch the old nun bow to her helpers all the way from the waist, an act of humility the like of which I have never seen. Then, using her stick, she turns around and bows to me and my own head is bowed in response. The men watch her enter a small building and insist on accompanying me around the corner to the convent.

I am drenched in sweat, and, in spite of the heat, as I walk into the square of the imposing turn-of-the-century yellow stone building, the convent of the sisters of St Joseph, I am shivering. Father David Newhouse is there waiting for me and he sees that I am in distress. 'Are you all right, Said? What's the problem?'

'Is there somewhere I can splash some water on my face, David?' and in five minutes I rejoin him in the small room full of unadorned, crudely made wooden furniture we had used for a previous meeting.

'It looks as if you had some excitement coming over here. What happened?'

I go through the story in detail, and David tells me that the old nun belongs to an Ethiopian Church nunnery next door and that the incident is one of many which have taken place lately.

'Are the incidents reported, David?'

'Yes. We reported two of them last week. It doesn't do any good. This convent and the Ethiopian nunnery are close to Mai Shairem, the area of the religious zealots. They don't want us here; it isn't anything organized, but they would rather that we leave and the youngster express the feeling of the elders through stupid acts like the one you've just witnessed.'

'So there is nothing to be done whatsoever?'

'Not really, this kind of thing is part of life here.'

'What about the old nun?'

'What about her?'

'Can anything be done to help her? Can anything be done to help the Ethiopian convent where she is?'

'Not really. There are so many things like this taking place. I am very sorry you had to be in the middle of it, and I am sure she's thankful, but that's as far as it will go.'

'I hate to be persistent, but was it because she was a nun or because she was black?'

'I don't know, it could have been either – or both. The important thing is that she obviously wasn't hurt.'

Random violence in the occupied territories isn't limited to teenagers and religious zealots. In fact most acts of violence are carried out by members of the Israeli Defence Forces (the Israeli army) and the Border Guards (the internal security organization). This is surprising since, to varying degrees, members of both forces are trained to avoid violence. What nobody can teach members of these or any other force is how to react to fear, how to behave under pressure.

I remember standing in front of Damascus Gate, the main entry and exit point to the old city, to watch the six-man Israeli patrol on guard there. I watched them for two hours as thousands of Arabs walked past them without saying a word but silently and unmistakeably telling them that they hated them. The soldiers on this duty are under orders to hold their rifles horizontal to the ground in a state of readiness which is supposed to guard against the unknown, unexpected attacker. I remember thinking that – under circumstances such as this – incidents of violence are inevitable. I still believe that, and I am thankful that soldiers don't go berserk more often and entertain us to more violence. But occasionally fear reigns supreme and its violent consequences are tragic.

I am in Ramallah to visit one of the patients at the Abu Raya Rehabilitation Centre, a Swedish Government-funded establishment which cares for disabled victims of the *intifada*. Said Bannoura, eighteen, is a victim of the indiscriminate fear and violence which envelops the occupied territories. All I know is that he was shot and seriously wounded under very peculiar circumstances and that, barring the performance of a highly experimental surgery which is not available locally, he is paralysed for life.

The Centre is slightly out of town, a three-storey building overlooking rolling hills full of olive, fig and citrus trees. The building itself is exceptionally clean and the entrance hall and reception desk subscribe to a remarkable sense of cleanliness and organization. I am introduced to Abadallah Bannoura, Said's father, a smiling, suntanned small man in his forties who is there to help with the interview. He greets me warmly and leads me to the second-floor recreation room where Said is waiting for us.

Said is obviously in pain and he moves his head from shoulder to shoulder and winces and I volunteer to terminate the interview, but both he and his father are insistent that it should proceed. They want the world to hear his story, what follows in his own words.

'I am from Beit Sahur [a known centre of Christian resistance to Israeli occupation, a little south of Bethlehem]. It all happened at 8 p.m. on 7 April 1991, when I was walking back home after playing with my mates. It was a little dark, yes somewhat dark. A little distance from our house, I ran into a contingent of Israeli Special Forces wearing Arab headdresses. They do that, they wander around incognito, but we can always tell who they are because they never get it right. They do this when they're trying to trap someone who's on the run, or when they go into Arab neighbourhoods.

'I started walking fast because I didn't want any trouble with them. A very short distance from our house, as I turned a corner, I came face to face with one of them, and there was nobody else there and I could tell he didn't expect to see me. I moved to avoid him, but he pulled out a gun. I froze and he panicked. He started shooting, and he wouldn't stop. I can't tell how many times he fired, but he wouldn't stop.

'Others, the colleagues of the man who shot me, came to see what had happened. I was on the ground for a long time. Two of them kicked me several times. Then they took me to Bassa Hospital and then to the Haddassah Hospital and there they discovered I had lost a lot of blood and put me through several emergency routines which I don't understand.

'That's when I was told that I had been hit five times, once in my chin, three times in the lungs . . . one bullet had shattered my spinal cord. I was kept at Haddassah for twenty days, including three days in intensive care, then I was released. I had a relapse and was readmitted to Makassed Hospital for two months, released again, then readmitted for another month and a half after which they arranged for me to come to the Rehabilitation Centre.

'I am here now. I go home at weekends, but I am here. Doctor David, he's a Swede, tells me there's a chance that I will walk again, but I don't know. They try to make us study and follow a constructive schedule and of course there are hours of physiotherapy that we have to go through. I am in pain a lot of time; the nerves in my back still hurt and that still affects me.'

I am impressed by Said's organized presentation of the ugly incident and its tragic consequences, and I continue the interview after he turns down another offer to terminate it.

'Said, what about the man who shot you? Have you heard anything about him?'

'No, I don't know much about that, maybe my father does. All I know is that they kept coming to interrogate me while I was in the hospital. People, security people, came five days in a row and they had a list with them and they were trying to determine whether I was one of the people on the list – I think it was a list of wanted people.'

I turn to the father and ask him whether he knows anything about the man who shot his son and he puts out his fourth cigarette and speaks, but only after he gives a smile of derision.

'The Israelis claim they don't know who the officer who shot Said is. It isn't only the usual coverup, there's more to it. They don't want the world to know that one of their officers panicked.'

I returned to Said. 'If it isn't too painful, tell me how you feel about what happened to you?'

'I am proud. This is a resistance wound, and I would do it again. I am not a hoodlum or a thief, I am a resister.'

'But wait, you said you were walking home, that you weren't doing anything else.'

'Yes, I was. But I am a resister and I believe that the man shot me because he recognized me from previous occasions when they, the security people, dispersed the boys of our school who were throwing stones at them. I have been stopped by the Special Services people before, and I do think the man who shot me recognized me.'

'I see, I see. What do you want to do now? What would you like to do with your life?'

'I want to continue my studies, go to a university, to study nursing or something like that. But it isn't possible yet because I suffer loss of memory because of the drugs I have to take.'

'I hope my next question won't offend you, but does your being a Christian matter in this situation? How do you and your Christian friends feel about being resisters?'

'I don't even know what you mean. Being a resister to Israeli rule has nothing to do with being Muslim or Christian, it has to do with being an Arab, a Palestinian. I am that and being Christian has nothing to do with things. In Beit Sahur, where I was shot, we have everything, all religions. The man who shot me didn't ask what religion I was before he did it. The men who came to the hospital to interrogate me in the hospital didn't care what religion I was.'

Once again I addressed myself to the chain-smoking father. 'Do you feel the same?'

'First, let me state that I am proud of Said; we're all proud of him. And I am proud of his brothers. My son Raed was detained for two months and Khalid was allowed to go to Germany on condition that he stay away for three years because he's a PLO supporter, and the young one Nabih is too young, but I hope that he will grow up the same way.'

This time, noticing that Said's pain appears to be getting worse, I do terminate the interview. I bid him a fond goodbye and promise to keep up with his case. The father and I take a service taxi back to Jerusalem. He continues to tell of how determined he and people like him are to transmit a message to the world.

'I am Christian, Greek Orthodox, but I can tell you that the world outside doesn't know how much we're suffering. Even the Arabs don't want to hear any more. We will, must continue to resist and expose Israeli policy to the world. As Said told you, their bullets don't discriminate and they do shoot Christian youngsters, don't they?'

Two days after my visit to Said Bannoura, on 23 September 1991, Zhogbi Zhogbi of the Middle East Council of Churches telephones to ask me to join him in a visit to 'a new teenage victim'. He picks me up in his car and we are on our way to St Joseph's French Hospital, a short distance from my hotel and from Zhogbi's office. We rush into the old building and Zhogbi leads the way to the second floor. We hurry down the corridor followed by Bill Warnock of the American human rights organization World Vision. Warnock was waiting for us in front of the hospital.

Zhogbi pushes the door gently and motions us to walk into the square 1920s solidly built room. There is a small, young woman in the corner with her hands in her lap and in bed, asleep and hooked to a drip, is Bishara Samir Zaballah. We use sign language and sit silently and I can see that the hidden part of Bishara's face is bandaged.

A nurse comes in and tells us it's time to wake him and she does. He turns round and opens his eyes and sees us, but he's still half asleep and in too much pain to say anything or register surprise. The little woman unfolds her hands and speaks.

'I'm his aunt; one of us is with him all the time. They wake him up regularly; there is a medical reason for it. I am glad you're here, somebody should know about this. The local newspapers couldn't report the incident because of local censorship, but they tell me that it has appeared in Italy and Abu Dhabi. We don't know, but we feel a crime like this should be reported.'

Bishara is moving in his bed trying to make himself comfortable and his aunt arranges the tubes out of his way and helps him with the pillow and he is finally fully awake.

Bill Warnock speaks first. 'How do you feel, Bishara?'

The patient winces as if trying to smile and his voice comes through grainy and slightly muffled, obviously affected by his bandaged head wounds.

'I'm all right now, much better, thank you.'

His aunt who finally gives her name as Mai tells us that it's easier for him to speak Arabic and that I should try to play translator.

'Bishara, if it is too painful for you to speak, then we'll come another time.'

'No, it's all right.'

'Mr Warnock is with an American organization which is concerned with cases like yours and I am a writer – I think you know Mr Zhogbi. If you can, please tell us what happened to you. Mr Zhogbi told us it is best if we hear it from you.'

He asks for his pillows to be readjusted and Zhogbi and his aunt accommodate him. He looks right at me, sitting at the foot of his bed. 'I was wounded on the 16th, a week ago. It happened in Bethlehem, 500 yards from Manger Square; that's where we live, in Bethlehem. It was early in the evening, after seven, maybe closer to eight.

'I was writing graffiti on the wall, slogans against the massacre of Sabra and Chatilla [two Palestinian refugee camps in Lebanon where several hundred Palestinians were massacred by anti-Palestinian Lebanese with the tacit approval of the nearby Israeli forces]. I had a spray can of paint and I was writing anti-Israeli slogans on the walls of the little square, the one next to Manger Square.

'Suddenly an Israeli army jeep with dimmed lights was coming towards me from one side. I dropped the spray can and wanted to run in the other direction but there was a jeep coming from that side. And four foot-soldiers were coming at me from right ahead. So there I was with my back to the wall and the can of paint on the ground, right next to me, and I couldn't think of anything to do so I raised my hands to surrender.

'The foot-soldiers were right in front of me, two yards away. One of them flashed a light in my face and another fired. It happened at the same time as I moved my head to avoid the light.

'I don't know what happened after that, but presently I came to and and I must have moved on the ground because a soldier kicked me with his boots. I kept going out and coming to, but I could tell no one was trying to move me. But then I was awake for a while and a soldier propped me up and told me to touch the blood on my face and cover the graffiti with it. I couldn't; I passed out again.

'When I woke up the following time, I was on the floor of a small army truck and they had taken my shirt off. One of the people with me in the back of the truck said something to the driver and the driver drove faster and moved from one side of the road to the other and I was rolling back and forth and screaming with pain and the soldiers were laughing.

'They stopped at Bassa, but before that they tied my head to my feet and I could see that I was bleeding. They tried to interrogate me, before administering first aid, and it was the man who flashed the light in my face; I could see him with the one eye I could use.

'I said to the officer, "Why did you shoot me? I surrendered." He told me that he didn't shoot me, but that if the other guy hadn't shot me then he would have shot HIM. They couldn't get much out of me because I kept passing out, so they took me to Haddassah Hospital.

'I really don't know what happened in Haddassah, but they told me that the operation to extract the bullets was three and a half hours long. My family transferred me here two days ago because Haddassah is expensive. The security people came to Haddassah to interrogate me. There wasn't much to tell them; I was writing slogans against what happened to the Palestinian refugees of Sabra and Chatilla.'

I finish my word-for-word translation of what Bishara tells me and Bill Warnock and I are shaking our heads in utter disbelief. I feel as if I am reciting a chapter of the book of hell.

'Gents, I don't care what anybody says, I've heard enough and I don't think the boy should be put through a question-and-answer session in his condition.' I say this, stand up to leave and Zhogbi and Warnock follow me. We pause in front of the hospital to express our horror to each other in totally inadequate words, and I ask them if anything is being done about the incident, if there is anything that can be done.

'We're going to follow up on this one,' says Warnock. 'We've retained Linda Beyer to handle it; she's a South African Jewish lawyer who's active in human rights campaigns and she's as horrified by this as we are. People from the UN and Al-Haq [a Palestinian civil rights group] have already been to see him. But there isn't much to do, though we will try. I promise you: we will try.'

On the way back to my hotel, I ask Zhogbi Zhogbi to provide me with Bishara's particulars. They read something like this: fourteen years old, one of four children, father UN employee, mother housewife, in his eighth year at Al-Amal school, a practising member of the Greek Orthodox church.

'What is your group going to do about it, Zhogbi, what does the Middle East Council of Churches do about cases like this?'

'We write reports, we write reports and send them to Christian groups who already know of hundreds of cases like this, and they probably throw them in their wastepaper baskets. Yes, that's what will happen.'

A LICENCE TO VISIT MR JESUS

'They stopped one of my tour guides near the Church of the Holy Sepulchre and asked him for his licence. He didn't have one, so they ordered him not to continue with the tour. The group of tourists with him protested saying that they needed him, but it was no use. The Israeli army officer who was in charge told the tourists that "a tour guide needs a licence to visit Mr Jesus" and our tour guide didn't have one. Can you imagine it? Only Jewish tour guides can visit Mr Jesus.'

This is a typical story of what is happening to the tourist business of the Holy Land. The speaker is Jabra Khanu, an Assyrian Christian and the owner of Guiding Star Tours, a forty-year-old travel company. The background to Abu Samaan's (as he is known) complaint is very simple. The law requires all tourist groups visiting the Holy Land to have guides licensed by the Israeli Government and the Israeli Ministry of Tourism hasn't licensed a single Arab tour guide since they occupied the West Bank and Gaza in 1967. People like Abu Samaan, determined as they are to stay in the business and maintain their Arab and Christian identity, resort to using unlicensed guides with obvious sad results which include the payment of heavy fines and warning of closures of their businesses.

As a result of the Israeli refusal to license Arab tour guides, and because licensing Jewish tour guides is a simple matter of procedure, the tourist business is moving from Palestinian Christian hands to Israeli hands. The tourist business has been the number-one industry of the Holy Land for most of the twentieth century and it has been Christian controlled for all of this time – a natural consequence of the fact that most of the tourists are Christians and come there to visit Christian shrines.

The slow transfer of the tourist business to Israeli hands through a process of attrition, the natural disappearance of all Arab tour guides licensed prior to 1967, may represent one of the most damaging economic acts against the Arabs of the occupied territories and it is definitely the one act which has affected the Christians to the extent of threatening their very existence. It is part of a deliberate, cruel attempt at economic strangulation and its immediate effects are as devastating as the widely known Israeli programme to expropriate Arab land.

Abu Samaan, the man who attaches so much importance to the story of his guide not being able to visit Mr Jesus, is a seventy-year-old man who has seen a lot in his life. He isn't the type to exaggerate a simple situation because it affects his business, but because others within and outside the territories miss the significance of it; even the media have devoted very little to this problem. He is angry and frustrated.

I am facing Abu Samaan, sitting across from him, in the back of his long open-plan office while his staff are shouting into their telephones, talking to associates all over the world, transmitting visit schedules, visa requirements and other information. It doesn't feel like the travel office of someone who's suffering, and the man's mature good looks and his beautifully tailored suit force a question as to how much damage Israeli discrimination has done to him.

'Don't be fooled by appearances, my friend. We've always been big and we're not going out of business. But left alone, without Israeli interference, I'd have a staff of sixty or more people instead of the nine I have now. And keep in mind that others who're not as well-established or financially strong have gone out of business. I'll go further: without Israeli interference the tourist business would change the economic situation of the West Bank, certainly we would be able to employ thousands more people. But they won't leave us alone, not a chance. Israel is a religious state which discriminates against all non-Jews; it is also a state which is broke and needs money, and tourism is one of the major sources of income here, if not the number-one source. Let me show you something which will tell you how much of a religious state Israel is. You'll see what I mean with your own eyes.'

Abu Samaan opens a drawer in his desk and pulls out what looks like a simple diary. 'This is a 1991 diary, a giveaway courtesy of the Israeli National Diamond Centre. Now look at the cover . . . here; it's a picture of the Third Temple. This is a picture of a design, a model of the proposed temple, and they intend to build it. It isn't exactly a secret when it is on the cover of a giveaway diary, is it? And there were some postcards with the same picture, but they have stopped selling them.

'You know Jerusalem . . . do you see where it is located? Yes, right where the Dome of the Rock is located today. They're going to raze the Dome of the Rock and construct the temple in its place. They don't give a damn about Muslim feelings, the one billion Muslims in the world don't matter, nobody matters to the Israelis except themselves. If they go ahead with this, and it will come to that sooner or later, then it will unleash one of the biggest religious wars in history. Every Muslim in the world is ready to die for the Dome of the Rock, but that won't stop them. Now, my friend, if the Israelis aren't worried about the feelings of a billion Muslims then they're not going to worry about what happens to a bunch of Christian tour operators who have no backing. Don't you agree?'

The incredibly provocative diary picture of the Third Temple renders me speechless. Abu Samaan's assessment is correct, millions of Muslims would be willing to die to stop the demolition of the Dome of the Rock. What I hear next makes things worse; Abu Samaan tells me that the Diamond Centre is an Israeli Government organization; in other words the reproduction of the model of the Third Temple has some official backing. We look at each other without saying a word and I decide to take the conversation back to the subject of the Christians and their problems.

'Abu Samaan, since we have so little time, we'd better stay with the Christians and the tourist business. What else besides refusing to license tour guides are the Israelis doing to take the tourist business out of Christian hands?'

'A lot. Among other things they even hamper the work of the few tour guides we have left; for example, our tour guides can't enter the airport and theirs can, so it looks as if they're offering a better service. Our tour buses can't enter some areas of the country, the areas in question change all the time. El Al, the Israeli airline, can offer better prices for Israeli-managed tours than we can get. Also, did you know that in order to work in this business in Jerusalem, that you have to be from Jerusalem. In other words we can't employ Arabs from the rest of the occupied territories which makes our life very difficult.

'It is an all-inclusive state of war on us in this business. I mean Israeli tour guides don't allow tourists in their care to eat in Arab restaurants, because the Arabs are supposed to be dirty and full of diseases. I don't know how to make lists, but they stop our buses from reaching Hebron and Nablus and their creeps are calling Jesus and the Virgin Mary bad names within earshot of us.'

We're on our third cup of coffee and Abu Samaan is issuing orders to his staff. Our conversation has him in a state of excitement. He is waiting for me to give him an opening to continue his onslaught.

'What do you do to counter all this, Abu Samaan?'

'First, let me make one very important point. If tourism dies, then we all die. If Israel succeeds in transferring all the tourist business from the Christians to their people, then the Christians here are finished. The arts and crafts, hotel and transportation businesses follow, are subsidiary to tourism.

'Now to your question. Believe me, we have tried and we continue to try. We formed the Christian National Committee and decided that tourism is our number-one concern. We retained Israeli lawyer Ahroun Sourik to deal with the problems facing us, the limitations being placed on us. He's a nice man, but he hasn't done much, can't do much. We have appealed to Christian groups throughout the world and we have even met with members of the Bundestag, the German parliament, but no one is willing to take issue with what the Israeli Government does or decrees. Nobody wants to be labelled anti-Semitic.

'It's working, believe me it's working, the Israeli policy to get rid of the Christians. There used to be 30,000 Armenians in Jerusalem – where are they? There used to be 50,000 Greek Orthodox, and they're gone as well. We contacted Billy Graham and asked for his help and got a lot of waffle in return. We have been in touch with the embassies of the US, UK, France and other countries and we have asked for their help, but we got nothing back. Their idea of helping us plays right into Israeli hands, they're willing to facilitate issuing emigration visas for some of us to leave this place. Yes, everybody's solution is to have us vanish, disappear, to bury the problem once and for all.'

I wait a while to give him a chance to catch his breath. He looks at me as if he is challenging me, and I want to keep him in this state of controllable anger and get the best out of him. Instinctively, I go to the second biggest problem – after the Israelis – facing the Christians of the Holy Land.

'What about the Muslim fundamentalist presence and the pressure that exerts? Has that scared tourists away or caused problems for tour operators who bring the Western people? People often wearing very little, I might add!'

He isn't angry with me, but clearly he's annoyed, and he adjusts his glasses, clasps his hands in front of him and leans towards me to tell me off in private.

'You're sounding like the rest of them; you want to create a diversion. We've had the problem with the Israelis since 1967 and it's getting worse and its results are right here for you to see and you want to talk to me about Islamic fundamentalism because people in the West like that. I am not going to help with your diversionary tactics. Our relations with our Muslim brothers have never been better; we have no problem there. They haven't done anything to hurt us, ever.

'Instead of this nonsensical Western question, you should concentrate on Israeli atrocities – and they're real. Why don't you write about how Israeli soldiers attacked a priest inside the Church of the Holy Sepulchre and how we Assyrians, one of the oldest churches in Christendom, can't conduct the procession of St Mark during the Easter festivities? I'll tell you why, it's because we have to pass between two Israeli settlements and we're afraid, and the reason we're afraid is because they've attacked us in the past and thrown shit on us. That stuff isn't reported, but the littlest problem with our Muslim brothers and you lot are off and running. Report the occupation, my friend, the occupation and its ugly reality. You know what an occupation like this does to people, it takes away their dignity and without your dignity you're not worth a damn. Write about the people who've taken our dignity away from us, and leave the Muslim fundamentalists alone.'

I like the angry man in front of me, particularly the way his hands were in front of him when he said dignity. I judged him to be a true believer, a decent Christian gentleman of the old school. His claim that the Muslim fundamentalist danger is exaggerated beyond its inherent menace is something with which I cannot agree, but the point that the occupation is the immediate problem is an argument that I do not dispute. Certainly, the damage being done by the Israelis is a more serious and immediate problem.

Abu Samaan continues. I hear of how the Israelis confiscated some of his land and how he waited several years to obtain a building permit to add to his house and never got one. As I had suspected, he finally admits to being involved in a number of charities and of contributing to them, regularly. It hasn't been an easy two and half hours, but they have indeed been very exciting and, after the usual apology and disclaimer, I ask Abu Samaan why he doesn't leave and retire to somewhere more peaceful. 'I am not going to leave. I am staying in Jerusalem. If we don't have loyalty to Jerusalem, then we're lost. I can't leave. I hope you understand that.'

We look into each other's eyes, and I know he means what he says and it's endearing. At the start of the interview he told me that everything he would say could stay on the record, that he was not afraid. I had not doubted that, but the depth of the commitment he had within him showed itself slowly, if angrily. Abu Samaan is not ashamed of what he is and the way he is. He is in love with Jerusalem. I try to reciprocate, to respond to his enchanting openness by wishing him God bless and by telling him that I find his love affair deeply touching and utterly grand.

The following day I got to see my friend Diana Safia who runs her family's business, Safia Travel. Diana who is acting as my mentor during this period of research knows the travel business and has no problem answering me. She confirms what Abu Samaan had told me. She elaborates on the tour-guide part by telling me that most of the Arab tour guides are getting too old to do the job, after all most of them were doing the same taxing job in 1967. Then she goes further and tells me how in the course of the Israeli campaign against the Arab presence in this business, normal competition tactics have assumed a particularly ugly way of expressing themselves. For example, the Israelis control *all* the tourist business which originates in Canada because their loyalists in that country have convinced the provincial Canadians that Arab tour companies are run by a bunch of thieves. 'A whole country has been lost to us, Said,' says Diana puffing on her cigarette. 'Who knows what's next?'

In conclusion Diana advises me to investigate the only case where people have got round the tour-guide requirement and limitation. I follow her advice and make an appointment to see Father Peter Mathes, the head of the Pilgrims' Office.

Father Peter Mathes isn't only German and a former Wehrmacht officer, he still walks with the stiffness and energy of a military man. He has been in Jerusalem for fourteen years and reports directly to the Papal Nuncio, in other words he is beholden directly to Rome and not to the local Roman Catholic church and its Patriarch. I meet Father Peter at Notre Dame, the headquarters of the Pilgrims Office and one of Jerusalem's best and most strategically located hotels. (For a moment I have a difficult time entering the place; my favourite uncle, Ali, was killed during an Arab attack on the building in 1948.)

He is a round man of about five foot seven and his hair is sleeked back and he speaks English impeccably but with a distinct German accent which owes nothing to the surroundings. The Father is in religious grey and short sleeves and he ushers me to the terrace where we sit in full view of the Mount of Olives and most of old Jerusalem. The people round us are speaking several languages; they appear to belong to the hotel part of Notre Dame.

Somehow our conversation begins with Father Peter making a long, outspoken and detailed statement about the position of Christianity in the Holy Land (see The Christians Against Themselves, p. 105). We talk about this for an hour and a half and only the time factor makes me turn to the specific business of tourism and how it affects the local Christians.

'Father, I understand you've overcome the Israeli requirement for tour guides which they use to squeeze the Christians out. How did you do that?'

'That, everybody wants to talk about that. Very simple really, but people here don't like simple things. We distinguished between tourists and pilgrims. We claimed, rightly of course, that pilgrims need religious guides to visit Christian places, so the guide can't be Jewish. Yes, how can that be when you're performing a Christian pilgrimage?' He laughs at his own ingenuity and I join him.

'I think I understand what you did, but could you give your own explanation in detail, I want to use your own words.'

'Right, not licensing Arab guides isn't a law, it is a Ministry of Tourism regulation which relies for its enforcement on some stupid laws which are on the books. It is essentially a regulation which they enforce rigidly, carry to absurd extremes. There was the case of the Arab who had lived in Spain for thirty years and he wanted to come here in the company of a Spanish tourist group and act as guide; you guessed it, they wouldn't let him, and to them his Spanish passport carried no weight. Let me tell you,' and he holds me in his pale blue eyes to make sure of the impact of his words, 'they can be stupid, really stupid and unimaginative. I mean it is so obvious that they're trying to take the tourist business out of the hands of the Arabs.'

'With this as background, what I did was to change the name and the official title of the groups who came here to see us – ones from Spain, Germany and other countries. I declared them pilgrims instead of tourists and gave them priests to do the work of guides. I mean a pilgrim does need a priest to take him around the holy places, don't you think?'

Father Peter's hands are in the air gesturing enthusiastically and he is laughing and so am I, but not nearly as hard.

'So you got around the problem that way?'

'No, no, not that simple, nothing is that simple here. The Ministry of Tourism tried to stop us, they came very close to arresting our priests, the ones playing tour guides. So we took the whole case to court. It went up and up until it reached the High Court. We won, we actually won, though it was a surprise. As a result we signed what I call the Notre Dame Agreement on 5 July 1981, we signed it right here.

'Naturally, we can only handle Roman Catholic pilgrims, but it isn't bad. Now, including ones which come with the tours from outside, I have 1,000 priests who can act as guides and have 1,500 pilgrim groups a year. The average size of each group is forty to fifty people, so we're talking about over 60,000 people a year. Not bad, the Notre Dame Agreement.'

'Of course not, it sounds very good. But what about regular tour companies? They can't do what you do, resort to using priests?'

'No, this is strictly a church agreement with the Ministry of Tourism, it doesn't affect the overall picture.'

'Father, forgive me, but it seems to me that your concerns and those of the Christian tour operators who are being pushed against the wall differ substantially. You're happy because you've converted tourists into pilgrims, but that doesn't do anything for the business of the operators. What concerns me is what the church is doing to help the tourist

industry which is the backbone of the economy of the West
Bank.'

'We are doing what we can.'

'Why doesn't the church adopt the case of the Christian
tour operators and try to help them?'

'That is a political decision, and it is too complicated.'

'Let me put it another way. The Christians of the Holy
Land, Roman Catholics and others, are suffering because of
what Israel is doing to them, to their main source of income.
As a matter of fact, they're disappearing because of Israeli
actions. Why don't you try to do something to help them
with their problem?'

He holds his arms akimbo and looks directly ahead
towards the Mount of Olives and the Christian shrines which
dot the landscape. It is a beautiful view.

'Very nice, don't you think?'

'Yes Father, very. It never ceases to work, I was born over
there, in Bethany, in the southern fold of the Mount of
Olives. How about my questions?'

'I agree with what you say. The biggest problem here is
the drain, people leaving, and the reason they're leaving is
because they have no work and they have no work because
the Israelis have taken some of it away. But this is a big
political problem for higher up.'

'Damn it to hell Father, your people, the Christians, are
suffering because of the discriminatory policies of the
Ministry of Tourism, if not of the whole damn Israeli
Government. But you're not terribly concerned with that,
certainly not with the real economic welfare of your local
flock, only in creating pilgrims instead of tourists. What
about the people here? What about the local Christians?'

'Mr Aburish, I've already told you a lot about conditions
here, a lot. But I am still not in a position to keep answering
the same questions which you keep repeating in different
ways.'

We fall silent and think of ways to get out of our
confrontation. We're saved by the arrival of a messenger
who tells Father Peter that they're waiting for him to
conduct the service. We shake hands and express our

awkwardness in strange uneasy gestures. He has no doubt that I am not satisfied with what I've heard.

I order myself another drink and begin to wonder whether Father Peter's attitude is a personal one or it is representative of that of the church. The thought that – as so many times throughout its history – the church is much more concerned with people's souls than their earthly welfare and everyday suffering disturbs me and I refuse to condone or even accept it.

Someone approaches my table and extends a hand and I wake up enough to recognize an old friend, Jamil Awad. 'Said, I have been waving at you for a few minutes, you look as if you're in the middle of a big problem.' I thank him for saving me from the useless exercise of trying to find instantaneous answers to centuries-old problems.

I am on my way to Bethlehem two days after my meeting with Father Peter. I want to continue my investigation into the tourist business, the universally accepted Israeli attempt to control it and the subsidiary effects on other businesses. My decision to spend time wih the owner of a tourist-goods store leads me to Angel Giacaman, a member of a Bethlehem family who have been prominent in the business since 1925.

I had been to the Giacaman shop before and had visited their famous olive-wood workshop. The store occupies a prized location right on Manger Square. It is crammed with olive-wood works, textiles, native clothing and dresses, assorted *objets d'art* and some unattractive plastic items. I was pleased to discover that I had met Angel before, but we still couldn't conduct an interview in the shop, not with tourists walking in and out, and we decided to meet at her house the following day.

It is a red stone house with green shutters and it commands a beautiful view of several miles. Angel is most welcoming and the only person there is her elderly mother who greets me with the heavy Bethlehem accent that I haven't heard for years, a way of speaking which lends itself to imitation and the odd unintended nuance. Angel serves an orange juice

followed by a Turkish coffee and does everything to make
me welcome while apologizing for the day before. Her
mother tells me that she had known an Aburish from
Bethany, a really big spender who is no longer around, but
she can't remember his name. Even the living room decor –
old-fashioned deep cushioned couches and wedding pictures
covering three generations – add to the relaxed, homey
atmosphere.

'Angel, what can you tell me about the state of the tourist
business?'

Angel is a big girl with a big voice and no make-up and she
laughs. 'If you phrase your question this way, then the
answer is nothing, because there isn't a tourist business any
more. It's dead.'

'Do you mean that?'

'Yes, of course I do.'

'Then tell me how it died.'

'Two related things killed it: Israeli pressure and the
consequences of the *intifada*. If you accept that the *intifada* was
the inevitable consequence of Israeli pressure then it is one
big thing, Israeli pressure.'

'Shall we start with the *intifada* first. Do you support it?'

'Hey, hey, don't go confusing what I am saying. Of course
I support the *intifada*, like every loyal Palestinian, but
that doesn't mean it doesn't have origins or economic
consequences.'

'Tell me about both, as you see them and as they have
affected your business.'

Her petite mother urges her to speak out and Angel
protests that she isn't afraid and leans across the coffee table
to face me.

'You know the *intifada* had to happen, I mean the Israeli
pressure was too much for over twenty years and our
dissatisfaction had to express itself and hence the *intifada*.
Israeli pressure, abuse, created the *intifada*.

'We support the *intifada*, emotionally and, in our case, in
practical terms. Our practical support means that we open
our shops for only half a day as an act of solidarity with the
children. We've been doing this for three years now, it has

affected our business substantially and the question is whether you can survive on half-time opening. I mean there are many occasions when there are tourists around and they go to Israeli-owned shops because the Arab-owned ones are all closed and the tourists just have to get what they need. And it isn't only that we're open for half a day, but very often we're forced to close for the whole day, again while the competition is open – much too often if you ask me.'

'Under what circumstances do you have to close for the whole day?'

'We have a lot of bomb scares in Manger Square and they, Israeli security people, close the whole square every time there is one; our national leadership calls one-day strikes at least twice a month; there are occasions when our youngsters throw stones at Israeli army patrols and the Israelis order the shops to shut, as they do when collaborators with the Israelis are killed by our people, something which is becoming frequent; lastly we have the regular holidays. Last month I had to close eight out of ten working days in a row. So even if tourists were flocking to the Holy Land – and they're not – we wouldn't be there to receive them.'

'This is true of you and other shop owners?'

'Yes, it is true of all who own the old quality shops around Manger Square. It's really true of everybody, but we get bomb scares more often, that's all.'

'The type of shop which is affected by this in Bethlehem is Christian, is it not?'

'Yes, they all are . . . no, no there is one small shop which isn't Christian, but basically all the others are.'

'And you're suffering because of the half-day and full-day closures which are the result of the *intifada* which is the result of Israeli occupation?'

'What do you think? Of course we are.'

Angel's mother confirms what Angel is saying in a simpler and very endearing way.

'Mr Aburish, she's with me all the time now. I used to tell her she was working too hard and not spending enough time at home. Now I wish she would get out of my hair.'

We all laugh and Angel slaps her thigh happily to show that she's enjoying herself.

'Now tell me about the direct Israeli pressure on the tourist business. What are they doing to take the business away from you?'

'To begin with, they try to keep tourists from coming to Bethlehem. The temerity of it all – trying to keep a tourist to the Holy Land from visiting Bethlehem! I have it from tourists themselves: the Israelis tell them that Bethlehem is unsafe, full of Arab terrorists, or they tell them the Church of the Nativity isn't worth seeing. Can you imagine that?

'Then the Israeli Government demands that we pay income tax in advance and the figures are always inflated. They don't do the same thing to Israeli-owned shops. It is a single case of being penalized because this business of paying taxes in advance adds to our operating costs. Even our export business is interfered with, the procedure to be followed in exporting goods is much more complicated than the one which the Israelis have to follow, another competitive edge.

'I don't know what to tell you; the most important people in a tourist operation are the tour guides and now most of them are Israelis and don't want to deal with us. They'd rather take tourists to Israeli-owned shops.'

'What kind of help do you need to overcome the discriminatory pressures against you?'

'Anything that would help us compete: all we want is to be able to do business on an equal basis. We know our business and can compete, believe me. If they'd let us, we would win.'

'Where do the tourists come from now?'

'The same old countries. The number of US tourists is down, but so is European tourism and here there are no Japanese to speak of. Remember one thing: before 1967 there were a lot of Arab Christians who came from Egypt, Syria, Lebanon and Iraq and this part of the business has disappeared altogether. Things are really bad.'

'Do the churches, Arab political groups, or any individuals try to give you help by working with the countries where the tourists come from?'

'I have already told you: nobody wants to know. Things

are getting worse and if they continue in this direction then we'll go out of business. Some people have already gone out of business.'

'What are the people who have gone out of business doing now?'

'They have left the country altogether. They've gone to America and South America and other places.'

'So people are emigrating?'

'What else can they do, if we can't make a living here and nobody is willing to help us?'

'Would you leave Bethlehem yourself?'

'I don't know, no, I don't think so. No, we've been in Bethlehem for ages. We can't leave, not unless we're forced to, but it is getting close to that.'

Angel Giacaman refuses to let me leave before giving me another coffee and some roasted almonds. She and her mother tell me that things have never been this bad, and they speak of how much time they devote to working with the Women's Union, a civic organization which has just started a museum of Bethlehem crafts. At the end they tell me that there are twice as many Bethlehemites abroad as there are in the city. The statistical relationship between the expatriates and the locals is becoming more lopsided every day.

As I look at my notes and listen to the tapes which cover my interviews with Abu Samaan, Father Peter and Angel Giacaman, it becomes clear to me that they have confirmed my worst suspicions. The Israelis are making a grab for the tourist and subsidiary businesses. Surely protest against Israeli discrimination cannot be withheld for fear of accusations of anti-Semitism. A Christian tour guide is inherently qualified to visit Mr Jesus.

A VILLAGE CALLED ABBOUD

'Abboud will not disappear; I promise you Abboud will not
disappear. The Crusaders wanted to destroy Abboud, and
they almost succeeded, yes they came very close. In the
eleventh century, when the Crusaders tried to destroy us,
Abboud had a population of 25,000 people and seven
churches, now we're 3,000 people on one church; so they met
with partial success, but never succeeded completely. And
the Israelis are trying to reduce us to nothing, to force us to
move out. They'll fail; there will always be a place called
Abboud.'

'Are you telling me that the Crusaders annihilated most of
the population of this Christian village and destroyed most of
its churches? Since this is news to most people then please
elaborate on this point.'

'It's very simple, the inhabitants of Abboud were Christian
Arabs who belonged to the Eastern churches and they
supported our leaders, Saladin and the others, against the
Western church which wanted to colonize us.'

'So there is a tradition of the people of this village being
against outsiders?'

'Yes, it has always been that way.'

The speaker is Abboud's headman and his significant
words come in a torrent and I find myself making notes while
reverently silent. I have arrived a mere five minutes before
these words are uttered. We're sitting on low, backless
wicker chairs in front of his stone house, and his wife, son,

daughter and daughter-in-law are there, sitting opposite us as if watching a performance. On stage is the visiting writer – myself, my friend, guide and helper who found Abboud as an example of mixed Christian–Muslim villages, Roula Amin, and the colourfully dressed headman, clad in Arab regalia and resembling the Muslim Arab of the deepest desert.

The *mukhtar* (headman) recognizes that his sweeping statements, historically true as they are, may be too heavy an opening even for our serious conversation. He smiles and asks whether I would like another cup of Turkish coffee. He issues his order for more coffee without waiting for my answer, speaks in the direction of the women with the ease of someone accustomed to command, and his young, Western-dressed daughter disappears to make it and returns with it in no time at all.

As drinking coffee is a ceremony to be savoured, Selim Anfous, better known as Abu Elias after his oldest son, returns to the subject of my visit and its purpose and how I come to have arrived at the village so late in the afternoon (4.00 p.m.). I turn to my friend Roula Amin, the initiator and eventual organizer of the trip, and ask her to explain and she obliges.

'We took a taxi from Ramallah. Said couldn't come except in the afternoon and, as you know, there are only two buses a day to Abboud, the last leaves Ramallah at one in the afternoon. I was afraid you'd be busy, Abu Elias, because I told you we'd be coming earlier, but there was no way to contact you, none.' My interest is roused, especially by the new fact that there was no way to contact the headman.

'Abu Elias, Roula has given me an idea of where the village is and some of the conditions which exist here, but I keep finding out new things all the time. Do you mind giving me an outline of Abboud, its people and the conditions which prevail here. Start where you like.'

Abu Elias slurps the rest of his Turkish coffee and smiles. His wife is an exceptionally attractive woman who wears Palestinian native dress but forgoes the headcover worn by Muslim women. She looks much younger than her years and watches his performance, along with the rest of his kin.

'I have no problem telling our story, Brother Said, after all, you're one of the very few people who are interested. The rest of the world doesn't care. I've already told you that we have 3,000 inhabitants, but what I didn't tell you is that this is a mixed village, sixty per cent Christian and forty per cent Muslim. It's been this way for centuries, and don't ask me why because I truly don't know. It is accepted by both sides that the headman is a Christian and the job has been in my family for a while, most of this century in fact. I think Roula told you where we are, only twenty-nine kilometres from Ramallah, though it is a treacherous winding road. But what she didn't tell you is that we're on the edge of the green line; we were barely in the West Bank before the 1967 War.

'I don't know what intrigued you in what Roula said, but it's true that no buses come here from Ramallah after one in the afternoon and there are none from the other side, and we don't have any telephones. We're cut off from both sides.'

'Not a single telephone?'

'Yes, none, I thought that was what intrigued you. And there is no chance of getting one either, at least that's what I've been told.'

'Let me get this straight, Abu Elias, after the bus arrives here in the afternoon, this village is cut off from the rest of the world, both the Arab world and the Israeli world?'

'Yes, essentially yes. There are some cars here and a few pick-up trucks and, if necessary, people can go to other places but they don't, the only time they do it is in cases of medical emergency and the like. As to outside visitors, nobody ever comes here, nobody has any reason to. The people of Abboud go to other places to look for work or when they have medical and other needs, but everything in terms of our contacts and communications with the outside world stops early in the afternoon.'

'Are you telling me that you're self-sufficient in Abboud, that you have everything you need?'

Abu Elias throws the edge of his *kufiya* over his shoulder and slaps his hands together in front of him in gestures aimed at attracting the attention of his audience. 'No, what I am saying is exactly the opposite. I am saying that we don't have anything because we can't afford anything. That's why there's no reason for people to come in and go out here. If this was a wealthy place that bought a lot of things then you'd have a regular bus service every hour on the hour and both the Arabs and the Israelis would come here on a regular basis to take our money away. Look around, look around, this a very attractive place, green with excellent olive and fig trees, much more attractive than Kuwait, and I've been to Kuwait. Everybody in the world goes to Kuwait because it has money, and the Kuwaitis go out to spend it, but we in Abboud have nothing.'

His wife, Umm Elias, gives his monologue full approval and adds to it. 'Forgive me, my brother, but it isn't only the people who want to make money who aren't interested in us, even the religious people don't care, and, my word of honour, I speak for both the Christians and the Muslims. The church isn't interested in us, no interest whatsoever, and nobody is trying to help our Muslim brothers either. Nobody cares.'

I nod agreement and wait a polite while before continuing. 'Abu Elias, Umm Elias, all of you, how does this village live? You're the headman, how do your people live and what are their conditions?'

He grunts, shuffles his feet, adjusts his headdress and moves heavily on top of his chair, but he still looks dignified and handsome, a true headman of an old village steeped in history.

'This is a farming community, a good one at that – certainly much better than a certain place called Bethany.' We all laugh heartily; the verbal twist which provided much needed relief to lighten the atmosphere was unexpected. 'We used to grow olives, figs, grapes and citrus fruits and we make some of the best olive oil in the land and export it to places as far away as Kuwait and Saudi Arabia. I'd be lying if I told you we were wealthy, but we were comfortable and lived happily, mostly off the land and with the remittances

from some of our people who went to work in the oil-rich
countries.

'Now we can't live off the land any more. We can't live
off the land because the Israelis have taken most of it from us;
they have expropriated our best land. The biggest land
confiscation order was a few months ago, on 25 August 1991,
when they took away about 7,000 donum [2,500 acres]. They
took away some land after that, and of course they've been
confiscating land for over fifteen years. And needless to say,
they take away our best land and leave us with the rest.'

The man is in pain and shows it by rubbing his hands over
his forehead in a gesture of despair, and the rest of us share his
agony. His son Nassim, a handsome young man in trousers
and a sports shirt, crosses and recrosses his legs several times
and makes clear he wants to speak but his mother and the rest
tell him to wait for his father to finish. Roula looks in my
direction to tell me to go along with what goes in the
household, that the rules of respect should be maintained.

'They take away the best land to farm it, is that it?'

'No, no, Brother Said, they take away the land to build
settlements on them. The last settlement is Beir Arieh, a
mere two and a half miles away, just over that hill, and they
keep expanding it and needing more land and so it goes.'

'So there isn't enough land for the people of Abboud to
farm.'

This time his smile is a broad one and it has the
attractiveness of being free of malice. There's a naughty
twinkle in his eyes and I soon discover why. 'I am very glad
you've finally got the picture. That's it, Brother Said, we
don't have enough money to farm.' I join everybody in
laughing over the obvious allusion to my slowness but state
that my writing function requires that I clarify the statement
to its bare meaning.

'How do you live then?'

'Do we? Nassim here says that we don't live, that we're
dying a slow death. I don't know about that, but, seriously,
things are getting bad, very bad and they're going to get
worse. Our diet is ruining us; we simply don't eat as well as
before, the frequency of meat dishes is decreasing, if not

disappearing. There is no food, not even grain, and rice is becoming scarce.'

'Take me through it bit by bit, please. How did land expropriation affect your diets?'

'Very simple . . . they took away the land, the most productive land we had, perhaps over sixty per cent of it, and we can't live off what is left, we just can't. And unless we earn money by selling our produce, then we don't have money to buy things and that includes other food beside what we grow. There were two other sources of income, the people who worked in Kuwait and other oil-rich countries and some of our people who, sadly, had to switch from farming to working as construction workers for the Israelis. Farming has been disappearing slowly, they've taken the land from us bit by bit, not all at once, in order not to attract attention to their crime against us. Then there was the Gulf War, and that was sudden. As a result of it, there is no work for Palestinians in the oil-producing countries, and our people who used to send us money from there are trying to survive themselves. The third source of income, working in construction for the Israelis, is also gone. Their construction work is down and they have their own people who are coming from Russia and other places and they have to give them jobs. The impact of these three things coming together hasn't hit us yet, but it will soon and we're on our way to real poverty. I don't want to mention names, but we've got hungry people already and we're going to have more very shortly. I can't remember real hunger in my lifetime and I am fifty-seven years old, but we're going to have real hunger.'

'Is this story known outside? Do people know what is happening to Abboud, in Abboud?'

'Yes, but it depends on what part of the story. As I told you some of the things happening to us are new and the combination of these things, the fact that they're taking place at the same time, has just happened, so I don't know how clearly outsiders see our problem.'

'Why don't we go through them, then? Let's go through the three causes of economic misery, and you tell me who knows about them and what they have done to help, if anything.'

The ladies go and come as they please, Nassim is chain-smoking and bouncing his crossed leg nervously and Roula, a researcher with the television network CNN, is listening studiously. It is about 6.00 p.m. and the unusually hot September sun is setting over the hills and the trees are casting gentle shadows. The Muslim call for prayer is followed by the ringing of church bells and in the street ahead of us there is no life. Night is on its way to Abboud and, except for the discomforting thoughts about empty stomachs, there is a sense of peace in the place. The village headman continues his story.

'Years ago, for a number of years after they occupied the West Bank in 1967, we had no problems with the Israelis, none. Being a farming community, we were hardly a resistance centre. All that changed when they started taking away our land, in '64 or '71, I don't know, sometime around that time.

'We couldn't believe it; it came out of nowhere. What they wanted, or more correctly announced they were taking, wasn't fallow land, or land for occasional farmers, no, it was land which supported people, in this case a whole community. I myself went to the military governor and spoke with him, told him that I thought the whole thing was a mistake. He told me it wasn't a mistake, and that was all he told me. Not a word more, not a word less.

'It was a completely new situation, so I asked several of the headmen of other villages what to do, and I followed their advice. I went to a lawyer in Ramallah, a man by the name of Ali Shkeirat. We told him of our problem and he and I went to see the authorities, once again. The Israelis laughed him off, they just didn't listen to him. He himself gave up and told me to go elsewhere.

'I went to see Felicia Langer [an Israeli left-wing lawyer who documented her eyewitness account of Israeli torture methods in her book *With My Own Eyes*]. Felicia accepted the case, but she wasn't very hopeful; she told us she had an idea what the Israelis were up to and that it would be difficult to win. She was right, the whole case fizzled away in a year or two. They kept the land.

'Now we have lawyer Aziz Shehadeh in Ramallah and he goes through the motions of lodging papers and other things, but nothing happens, nothing ever happens. And with our economic situation the way it is, we simply don't have money to pay him, so the whole thing is frozen, in limbo, not that having an active lawyer would have done any good.

'Brother Said, I hate to say this because it sounds as if I differentiate, but the land the Israelis took, eighty-five per cent of it belongs to Christian families. You see the Christians have been here longest and had the best land and that's what the Israelis wanted, the best land.

'Most of our young people are unemployed; there's nothing to do, not a thing to do.'

'Tell me about that, tell me about the expatriates in Kuwait and other countries who used to send you money.'

'We had over a hundred of them. Some were educated – engineers and the like – and others were in simpler jobs. They made a lot of money working in Saudi Arabia, Kuwait, Qatar and the Emirates and they used to send money back to their families who spent it and kept the place going. I'd say they supported about five hundred of our people, a good number in this small population.

'Now, after the Gulf War, nobody wants them in their countries any more. They don't like the Palestinians because we supported Saddam Hussein, and these countries are deporting our people to places where there are no jobs, Jordan. So this source of income has dried up, completely. As a matter of fact it has resulted in some sad situations. The families of some of the people who worked in the Gulf would come back here but they can't, because their immigration papers aren't right, so some family members come back here while the others stay in Jordan.

'The whole thing is a piece of nonsense. How do you tell someone who was born here that he can't return, but the Israelis are shameless and they do it – and all the time.'

I look up from my notebook to find most of the audience listening impassively. What I am hearing is something they know, but that doesn't make it easier on them, and they support the headman's statements by mentioning the names of people stranded in Amman and other former Abboud residents who no longer have a place to live, let alone work.

'And the third source of income, Abu Elias, what happened to that?'

'In fact, that's a much simpler story. Painful as it was for them to do after their land was confiscated, some of our boys who were farmers turned to manual labour and started working for the Israelis to build the settlements in order to live. Just imagine the situation: the Israelis confiscate your land to build a settlement and you're reduced to working on it as a labourer, to build a house for someone who has taken your land from you. Anyway, they did, they swallowed their honour and their pride and they did it. The Israelis used to come to the village and collect them in trucks, like sheep, and take them to work. The numbers changed regularly, but they still employed a good number of people who had an income and enough to eat.

'Now the Israelis have their own people, the ones who have come here from Russia and other places and they use them instead. So our boys don't even have the demeaning work to perform. This just happened, and slowly we're going to run out of food and other things and there is going to be hunger. That's what I meant by a situation of real hunger.'

'Does anybody provide you with help? Do you receive any help whatsoever?'

'Yes, from one source only, from UNRWA [the United Nations Relief and Work Agency]. They're not supposed to help us because we aren't refugees, but they do, in a small way. They provide us with some grain. I am not scoffing at it because it is desperately needed.'

'What else is happening here?'

'Let Nassim tell you; everything else is happening here, everything which goes into the making of a disaster.'

I am glad to be turning to Nassim and the change from the headman provides a natural break and Abu Elias orders some mint tea for us. Nassim puffs on his cigarette and puts his index finger through his moustache to prepare for delivering his lines. His mother decides to do some coaching and she asks him to tell me what happened to him and his two brothers.

'All three of us have spent time in Israeli jails and detention camps. One time I was in for nine months and the second time I was in for twenty-four months, two years. My brothers were in one time each. The accusation is always the same, they tell us tht we work for the PLO which is an illegal organization. It doesn't do much good to get a lawyer because they claim they have inside information and they can't reveal the source. (The testimony of unnamed informers is accepted by the Israeli military courts.)

'My brother married his wife Lima while he was on the run, while the Israelis were looking for him to arrest him. We held the wedding in a church, a big church in Bir Zeit, and we had about sixty people on the lookout for Israeli patrols. We had a priest's outfit ready for him to wear in case the Israelis intervened up, but thank God they didn't and he and Lima managed to have a church wedding.

'He couldn't give Lima anything, he'd been unemployed and on the run for over a year and a half and completely broke, but he was determined to have a church wedding and we were determined to give him one. There was a lookout who spent the whole time of the ceremony in the church tower, and he was supposed to ring the bell the moment he saw the Israelis coming, but as I said they never came. They didn't catch my brother until a few months later and they sentenced him to nine months.'

Lima was the daughter-in-law who was with us. A pretty woman in a simple shift who shyly looked at the ground, she sat opposite her friend Roula Amin. I looked in her direction in an attempt to get her comments, but she said nothing. She wore a smile of pride and defiance, and the thought which came to me had to do with her telling the story of her wedding to her grandchildren.

'Nassim, let's put aside what the Israelis did to you and your brothers, do people here belong to political organizations?'

'Yes.'

'Is it all right to tell me about them?'

Another cigarette is lit, and Nassim takes a deep drag. 'With the conditions which surround us, everybody here is

political, I mean how can you avoid it when everything that
happens around you is political. There are several groups
here. The biggest is Fatah [Yasser Arafat's moderate wing of
the PLO] – and it is the biggest group – and the PFLP
[Popular Front for the Liberation of Palestine, headed by the
radical Christian George Habbash]; and there is the Muslim
movement Hammas, very small; and there are the communists, a moderate branch which relates to communists in
Western Europe. In reality most people follow Fatah and
Arafat.'

'What do they want?'

'Basically all the political groups want the same thing.
First they want the land confiscation to stop and then they
want the Israelis to give us back what they took away from us
and leave us alone.'

'Do you do anything against the Israelis? Is this active
resistance?'

'I can't tell you a great deal about this, but yes, people do,
the people who belong do. Youngsters attack the Israeli
settlements during the night, almost every night, and the
Israelis retaliate by coming into the village and arresting
people, as many as twenty at a time.'

'What kind of attacks do the youngsters mount against the
Israeli settlements?'

'Stones, they attack them with stones. They have nothing
else, can do nothing else.'

'And they think it's worth it to attack with stones and face
the possibility of imprisonment?'

'Obviously yes. They have been doing it for years and they
continue to do it in spite of the number of arrests. Some of the
people involved have been arrested and imprisoned several
times. It doesn't stop them, not even beatings and torture can
stop them.'

'So what we have in Abboud or near it is an *intifada* type
political confrontation with the Israelis, the economic results
of land expropriation and lack of work in Israeli settlements
and on top of that the economic effects of the Gulf War. Is
that it?' Nassim looks at his father to obtain his concurrence

with what he is going to say, but the headman uses this as an opening to return to centre stage.

'Not only these things, nobody cares about us, nobody is trying to help us to continue. I mean life here is becoming impossible, people are in a state of constant depression.'

I look at Roula Amin and can't help myself and I blurt, 'No exit.' She nods her head in sad agreement.

'Abu Elias, do tell me about a typical day in the life of Abboud, what happens here during an average day?'

He looks at his wife, then his son, then he turns to the rest of his family and he opens his hand and moves it across as if to an audience. 'They can tell you what happens here.'

My eyes focus on the handsome face of Umm Elias and I repeat the question.

'Nothing happens here, my brother, nothing. In the morning those who still have land go to work it, but their numbers are growing smaller all the time. Then there are some, fewer and fewer, who go to work for the Israelis or as far away as Ramallah. The rest of us repeat the same stories we tell every day; the only thing new is who got arrested the night before or something like that. The doctor comes two days a week and he doesn't have enough time to treat all the people who need treatment. Most of our people are suffering from diabetes and new diseases and the doctor says it's because of their diets. The Red Cross has been here several times, but their people say they can't help us, or don't have money to help us. I don't know; I am talking too much.'

Umm Elias makes us laugh and as she joins in her very pretty looks are marred by the fact that most of her teeth are missing and I resist the temptation to ask her why she doesn't have false teeth. Nassim lights another cigarette and decides to add to his mother's statement.

'The only outsiders who come here on a regular basis are the doctor and the garbage truck.' His hand touches his moustache again and it is obvious that he's trying to add to the light touch started by his mother. 'The driver of the garbage truck which serves Abboud and three neighbouring villages is one of our sources of news. People always have something new to talk about after he collects the garbage and we know where it comes from and accept it as gospel.'

Again everybody laughs, and the women cover their mouths with their hands in a gesture typical of women in this part of the world when they try to show some modesty. The conversation reflects the situation of Abboud; it is going nowhere and I decide to resort to simple direct questioning.

'What are your contacts with Palestinian leadership in the West Bank? I know they don't have much money, but they have some. Do they help you?'

Everybody looks at Abu Elias, and he answers. 'They don't come here, and we don't have any contact with them.'

'But why? They go to other places and try to help. The least they do is appoint lawyers when the land of a village is confiscated but they haven't done it in this case.'

'Believe me, nobody comes here. We're what you might call an out-of-the-way place, and they go to places which are in the limelight, where they might get some publicity out of trying to help.'

'And that's true of the church as well?'

He didn't mean to say it, but Nassim's words cut through the air like a bullet. 'What damn church? What church? We're Greek Orthodox here, and nobody from the church, any church, has come to see us in years. And this has other effects because the Red Crescent don't come here either, as they consider Abboud a Christian village and think Christian groups should take care of us. I think the church, all churches, should be ashamed of themselves. Their Christian brothers are near starvation and they do nothing, not a thing. I'll take you around the village and you ask people when was the last time we saw someone who belonged to a Christian group outside. Not for years.'

'What about the PLO or their people?'

'We've already mentioned that, they don't come to visit out-of-the-way places which don't provide them with publicity for whatever they do.'

'Not even aid organizations?'

'Not even them. We keep hearing about the EEC

providing help, but we don't get any of it. I wish you'd tell them that their aid should be directed at the people.'

'Right, but your Muslim villagers suffer equally?'

'Yes, nobody takes care of them either.'

'What are your relations with them? Do you get along or has the Islamic fundamentalist movement affected things?'

Once again Abu Elias is the focus of attention, the man entrusted with making what amounts to policy statements. 'Our relations with our Muslim brothers are good. The Israelis tried to get them to replace me because I am Christian, but they refused to comply and they came to see me and told me about it. In a gesture of national unity we held joint Christian-Muslim weddings with them and everybody participated and enjoyed themselves. Muslim fundamentalism hasn't touched us here, also because we're isolated. Our relations with our Muslim brothers are the same as they have been for the past ten centuries.'

I folded my notebook and thanked everybody around me and Roula and I looked at each other while thinking of the same thing: how do we get out of here? How do we get back to Ramallah and from there to Jerusalem? Abu Elias saw us wondering and laughed. 'No, you're not stuck in the middle of nowhere, we've already organized a small car to take you back.'

We leave after saying our long and fond goodbyes. Nassim walks us to the cars and invites us back to vist them to meet other villagers and I promise to try and come again. The dust-covered car is dusty inside too, an old Peugeot which grunts into gear with difficulty. The headman and his family wave at us and we wave back.

The car climbs the winding road out of Abboud and at eight in the evening I am still able to see olive and fig trees and vineyards. As the car reaches the top of the hill, I notice a strategically located Israeli settlement and there are settlers walking towards it with rifles on their shoulders. There is something absurd about them; they look completely out of place, like an alien presence. I look back to have a last glimpse of Abboud and I see a few stone houses, simple structures similar to those that have existed there down all the centuries, but there is very little light coming out of them. 'Roula, I hope he's right, I hoppe there will always be an Abboud, but I am not so sure. Those settlers look like people who like to have it their way.'

THE PROSPECT OF A HAUNTED HOUSE

'Let's be realistic, Said, by the turn of the century or a short time after there won't be any Christians left here. They will have all emigrated and they will be all over the world talking about an imaginary Palestine.' Camille Nassar, the energetic head of the YMCA believes he's making a realistic statement. By committing himself to the YMCA and subsidiary aid organizations, he is doing everything within his powers to prove himself wrong, but he thinks the tide is running against him and that the emigration of the Christians will continue until they disappear.

The less passionate Bernard Sabella, a Roman Catholic professor at Bethlehem University and probably the leading authority on Christian emigration from the Holy Land, is less pessimistic. 'Oh, there will be a Christian presence in the Holy Land; this is not the point really. The issue is what kind of presence, how big, small, integrated, local or foreign it will be. Having a single church is a Christian presence, but is it acceptable?'

Canon Naim Ateeq occupies the middle ground. 'Our people are leaving, and it is accelerating. We must do something to stop emigration as soon as we can – now, not tomorrow or the day after. The danger point has been reached, though there is still room for action.'

All three are agreed that emigration poses the greatest danger to the Christians of the Holy Land. They were not alone, their opinions were shared by every one of the eighty-four people I interviewed for this book. Religious leaders, politicians, businessmen, lawyers, professors, doctors, mechanics, shopowners, students, village headmen and others support them. Like Ateeq, the Christian community of the Holy Land realizes that emigration has reduced its presence to a dangerous level and that immediate remedial action is needed. Most people share the apocalyptic views of Camille Nassar.

The reality of the problem has prompted the heads of the Roman Catholic, Greek Orthodox and Anglican churches to petition the Jerusalem consulates of the United States, Canada, Australia and other countries to stop facilitating the issue of emigration visas to their dwindling faithful. This rare unified Christian act demonstrates the gravity of the situation; the feuding churches have had a tendency to subordinate their welfare to selfish jealousies and have very seldom acted together. So far this appeal has had no effect, the concerned consulates continue to issue visas for 'humanitarian reasons'.

Even Bernard Sabella's optimism evaporates in the heat of what he has uncovered by his own studies. His latest excellent study of Christian emigration contains two unhappy facts which augur poorly for the continued Christian presence he hopes for. The intention to emigrate among Palestinian Christians is highest among educated males of the twenty- to twenty-four-year-old age group. And the study confirms what I have heard and seen for myself: Christianity in the Holy Land has already been reduced to old men, women, churches and monuments. The oft-repeated jarring description of museum Christianity is not an exaggeration, it is aptly applied – all one has to do to validate it is compare the great number of churches with the small number of parishioners.

The process of emigrating, leaving, escaping, looking for work elsewhere or whatever name people might give the fact of Christian disappearance has been going on for a long time but everything supports the thesis that a crisis point has been reached. The Christians of the occupied territories of the West Bank and Gaza are down to a numerically insignificant three per cent of the population, compared with ten per cent in 1967, when Israel occupied the territories, and over twelve per cent in 1948, at the time of the first Arab-Israeli war.

David Newhouse, a leading authority on the Christians of the occupied territories, sees emigration as the most attractive of three evil options open to the subjects of his studies. 'They can go for seclusion, the creation of ghettos, but that is a less attractive alternative, especially for people who strongly feel they belong to the land. It would represent an unacceptable change in direction. Then there is the possibility of a life of delusion, a belief in pan-Arabism and the hope that the Arabs would eventually do something for them. With conditions in the Arab world the way they are, this is no more than a die-hard stance which is becoming less palatable by the day. (During this century, the Palestinian Christians did produce a disproportionately high share of political leaders and thinkers.) And there is emigration. With all the difficulties inherent in the act of emigrating, it is still the easiest and in many ways the most sensible way out.'

David Newhouse doesn't know Camille Nassar, but they share a common realism and an unattractive living reality. Their difficult to refute statements about the prospects for the Christians prompt me to reexamine and rehash the major problems behind Christian emigration:

The Israeli occupation and consequent denial of political and economic rights including their effects on education.

The Islamic fundamentalist resurgence and the constraints on the Christian way of life.

The lack of overall economic opportunity and the resulting high unemployment.

I use David Newhouse's impressive analysis for further conversation with Bernard Sabella. 'Bernard, what are the reasons people give for emigrating or wanting to emigrate?'

'They're the obvious ones, lack of work is definitely top of the list. Of course you must take into consideration that it has been going on for some time and this means they have no hope for the future. Worry about the education of their children is a close second. Thirdly, there is the apparent ease of it, the fact that Western consulates do give them visas to leave, this makes emigration an easy way out.'

'Are the consulates favouring the Christians or targeting them?'

Bernard smiles, knowing that the figures in his own studies suggest that. 'No, not at all. But the consulates are in the business of issuing visas to educated people and those who can assimilate and the Christians qualify more than others. Also many of the emigrants have relations all over the world, from earlier this century and other times.' (There are thriving Palestinian communities in the United States, Canada, Australia, Chili and other parts of South and Central America.)

Bernard once again proceeds to articulate depressing facts and figures behind Christian emigration. 'No exact figure of the number of unemployed exists, but it is somewhere around a staggering thirty per cent of the Christian population. Children's education is suffering very badly because of the Israeli closure of schools, and qualitatively because of the traumatization due to violence. And let's not forget that many good teachers who can get employment elsewhere have left. In addition to the attitude of Western consulates, Palestinian Christians in the US, South America, Australia, Canada and other places help their relatives emigrate. Palestine exiles' reasons for helping with emigration are the same as those of Western consulates, they'd rather see people leave than suffer. I find it difficult to take issue with either group.'

Jeannne Kattan, a professor of English at Bethlehem University and as such Bernard's colleague, a passionately committed Palestinian and Christian, has her own way of reducing Bernard's points to flesh and blood. She stares out of the window of her small office and points to an attractive young man in the courtyard. 'Do you see him? He's very bright and he has a BA degree in the arts. He can't find a suitable job, so he's taken a job as a labourer. He's got to eat. I won't even tell you his name, it's too embarrassing for him to have his name mentioned. And this is not an isolated example, there are many like him.' We both agree that the young man's continued presence is a triumph of commitment over circumstances and have no doubt that he would do much better somewhere else. Others have.

But Jeanne's humane, heart-felt attitude isn't shared everywhere. It is substantially different from the wish of the heads of the churches to keep everybody from emigrating without taking concrete steps to eliminate or ease the conditions which lead to emigration, even the formation of permanent study groups seems to elude them. Nor is the young man's predicament totally understood by people like Jireyes Said Khoury of Al-Liqa who reaches for the traditional Arab excuse and puts the whole blame on the Western consulates and Israel. He claims that, 'Israel makes it possible for people to leave, yes it suits their policies.' That Israel's repression policies are the major contributors to emigration is beyond doubt, but they are not applied exclusively to the Christians. Khoury is full of sound necessary plans to tell the world about the plight of the local Christians, but he is short on suggestions as to what to do with BA-equipped labourers.

My various conversations on the subject tell me that the time to talk to emigrants and would-be emigrants has come. It takes some effort to find some who are willing to discuss the subject. There is a bit of shame attached to leaving or thinking about it which fits into the picture of Palestinian Christians being a proud lot with deep-rooted attachment to their country.

I am with Rami Meo three weeks after he has got his emigrant's visa for Australia. He is thirty-four, handsome and a graduate of Birzeit University and the American University at Cairo. He taught Middle Eastern studies at Birzeit for two years and left to manage the family business, a quality antique shop near Jerusalem's Jaffa Gate which his great-grandfather started in 1872.

We meet at the National Hotel at 6.00 p.m. after a long

telephone conversation in which I managed to overcome Rami's initial reluctance to submit to an interview. Rami's three-year-old daughter is with him and her presence is an inadvertent reminder of some of the reasons behind his move.

Greetings out of the way, he starts apologetically. 'I have performed my duty, at least I have tried. Teaching young people is contributing, I believe it is. I enjoyed teaching, though it is financially unrewarding.'

'I agree with you. But let's go to the heart of the matter. How did you arrive at the decision to leave?'

'Don't think it was easy, as a matter of fact it was very difficult. My wife and I discussed it for over two years.' He smiles and continues. 'My wife taught with me at Birzeit; she's the type of woman who participates in family decisions. Yes, it was two long agonizing years before we finally decided we must leave. The children and worry about their future tipped the scale; we have a small boy besides this one. We're going to Sydney, and we're doing it for a simple overriding reason: to lead a normal life. We don't know what a normal life is. Just look at the past fifty years or so, when did we have a normal atmosphere during all that time? Never, never for a moment of my life. Our lives have consisted of worry about wars and uprisings and their consequences. A few months back, on 8 June, there were two bombs near the antique shop. Business came to a halt because people were scared to go there for a while. Do you call that a normal life? I think it is normal that we crave a normal life.'

'So you're talking about the economic pressures and their influence on your decision?'

'Of course, yes. Look at the past three years . . . they've been a huge financial disaster for a shop like ours. There was very little income and zero profit, and I mean zero profit. I mean how can one live? The only people who thrive in an atmosphere like this are politicians, gunrunners and revolutionaries – and I don't qualify. But it isn't only the economic factor, there is an absence of security. By security I don't mean the type which is changed by having bodyguards or other forms of protection against bodily harm, I mean it in a more spacious sense, the security of being. The Israelis don't give a damn about us, our leaders aren't terribly concerned with our welfare unless it helps their positions and the church hasn't succeeded in providing a sense of belonging or security. It's all falling down, mostly on the heads of innocent people.'

'You mentioned the Israeli and economic pressure and the failure of leadership, but what about the pressure from Islamic fundamentalism?'

'Look, I am a loyal Palestinian, I feel I belong to the Palestinian state. The Palestinian state is an idea, to me an attractive idea which we need, but unfortunately this idea hasn't protected me or helped me. It can't protect my life against Israeli criminality, economic pressures, Islamic fundamentalist nonsense or anything. Do you get the drift of what I am saying? What I believe in, and want to continue to believe in, the idea of a Palestinian state, can't protect my life property, my simple being or anything. One more vital point: Is that state in which I believe about to emerge in any real form to change this picture?'

I decline to comment and wait for Rami's answer, but he needs to hear me on the subject. I admit that a functioning Palestinian state isn't on the cards, not in the immediate future.

'Right, then who's going to protect me and look after my interests? I can't rely on the Meo family; we're only six people, hardly a tribe. And certainly an impotent, stupid church can't do that. The church isn't concerned with that, its main concern is to make people Western or acceptable in a Western way. They equate that with an antiquated civilizing mission. They have nothing to offer me, I'm already there, I'm the product of Western education.'

'So in the absence of someone to protect you, you're leaving.'

'Yes, but I mean protect in the larger sense of the word, someone who would give me a sense of belonging. This emigration may not be permanent – who knows?'

'Are you saying you'd come back if circumstances change?'

'If they change in the direction I have been talking about, yes, most definitely yes.'

'What is going to happen to the antique shop – after all, it's part of the Jerusalem scene?'

'My sister will manage it and try to keep it going. Keep your fingers crossed.'

'And what will you do in Australia? Do you have something specific in mind?'

'I have no idea, I simply don't know. Maybe I'll go back to a university and get a PhD, or something else, something normal, very very normal.'

There is something elementally sad about Rami Meo's story; in a way his fear is more profound than a temporary one involving being attacked or needing a job. It is also sad because his undoubted talents are obvious, as is his love for his daughter. Watching him play with her confirmed to me that she's part of the complicated equation. Her presence, intentional or not, provided the right background to her father's tragic decision.

My meetings with the emigrant and others whose situations he articulates leave me angry, but I can't decide who should receive the brunt of my anger. My anger with the Israelis is too deep rooted and well established to need a new stimulus. I have been an eyewitness to their brutality for a number of years and I know that they welcome anything which plays into their hands, regardless of the human cost. I direct my anger at the churches, especially the wealthy one that can do most, the Roman Catholic church.

'Why,' I ask Father Peter Du Brul SJ, an instructor at Bethlehem University, 'why doesn't the church do more for the Christians of the Holy Land? Even helping the Catholics would do.'

'Mr Aburish, you appear to be looking for an illusive answer. The answer is not terribly illusive, the church is busy with problems closer to home, problems in east Europe and indeed problems which involve greater numbers of Roman Catholics than we have here. It as simple as that.'

'Wait a minute, father, the problem of the local Christians has been going for ages and most of the problems of east

Europe are relatively new. Why wasn't something done before?'

'I think you miss most of my point. The church has to worry about its followers all over the world. In addition to Europe, there are problems in South America, in South East Asia and many other places. Far be it for me to try to diminish the local problem, but some of the other problems are big. What I am trying to say is that you should view the problem here comparatively.'

As in previous meetings with other members of the Roman Catholic church, the father and I disagree on the role of the church and whether it has an obligation to address the immediate problems facing the community rather than administer to their scarred souls. In spite of our disagreement, Father Du Brul kindly gives me a copy of his book, *The Burning Tree, The Crisis of The Palestinian Christians.* I read the book the following day. My suspicions are confirmed, the church remains committed to an impractical spirituality. There is a great deal in the book about the meaning of suffering as an enlarging Christian experience and very little about Christians doing anything to stop emigration.

It takes a very long time for me to induce the member of a foreign consulate to speak to me to answer the accusations that their policies are aiding Israeli plans to get rid of the greatest number of Palestinians, including Christians. The young civil servant who belongs to one of the accused countries agrees to cooperate under conditions of anonymity.

'Tell me, are you aiding and abetting Christian emigration? By that I mean is it policy?'

'No, certainly not, that's utter nonsense.'

'Well, the figures are clear and they show that there's disproportionate number of Christians among those to whom you issue visas. What do you have to say about that?'

'There's no mystery there, I mean I hate to tell you that you haven't discovered anything. We don't discriminate on the basis of religion, but there's a bias in favour of educated people and those who already have relatives in our country. The Christians are more educated and many of them have relatives. It's a process of natural selection or something like that, but not religious discrimination.'

'So you're granting visas to them as Palestinians. Is that right? When it plays into the hands of the Israelis.'

'Yes, it is. This is nonsense, really. Do you wish us to stop issuing visas? Do you? There are certain things which have to be done to help and very often they supersede the basic national interests. I'll give you a more serious example. Arab workers go to work in Israel proper, for Israelis, and they do that because they have to live, to eat. The Palestinian leadership knows all about this, doesn't like it but has never done anything to stop it; they haven't even recommended to workers to stop crossing into Israel. It's simple, the workers need to eat, and so do the people who leave this country.'

'I see what you're saying and I am in basic sympathy with it, but the Christians have become an endangered species.'

'That's a good point, a very good point. I don't know what we can do about that. It's very sensitive any way you look at it, and I am sure you wouldn't want to make the decision concerning this.'

The rest of the interview revolves around the same point; to the junior diplomat, accommodating Palestinian Christian emigration is a humanitarian act.

A week after seeing Rami Meo and talking to Father Du Brul and the junior diplomat I go to Ramallah to meet Maurice Abdallah Nassar. We meet at the house of a mutual friend and Maurice, thirty-six and over six foot tall, walks in shyly in an old brown suit. The most striking thing about him is his old-fashioned good manners which show in everything from the way he insists on lighting people's cigarettes to the way he listens attentively, and he reminds me of films about the Second World War, ones with characters who have been seen better days and insist on airs and graces.

Unlike Rami Meo, Maurice isn't emigrating, but he is one of the thousands of Christians who're considering leaving, the ones whose departure might lead to a total Christian disappearance.

'The only things keeping me here are the children, if it weren't for the problem of readjustment they'd have to go through then I'd leave like a shot. I have five children, three girls and two boys, and three of them are in their early teens, the most difficult time. I may still leave. I think about it all the time.

'In addition to all the problems which you've undoubtedly heard about, I don't have any friends any more. My friends have all emigrated, they're in Canada and Australia and other places. Some of them have written to tell me how well they're doing and invited me to join them. That makes it more difficult for me to stay here. We'll see.'

'Our mutual friend and host tells me you're a motor mechanic. How did that happen?'

Maurice assumes I know more about him than I do and considers the reference to his job a reprimand. 'It's a trade, why not? I am a graduate of the University of Cincinnatti, but you can't do much with a bachelor's degree. It's of no use here, there's a surplus of them, too many degrees for the jobs available. I don't mind being a mechanic, I like the work.'

'How is it going? How's business?'

'Terrible, just terrible. Because of the *intifada* we work only four hours a day, which is not enough. But that's half of the story, and the other half is the all-day strikes you get all the time. In fact, according to my calculations, I've worked only one year during the past four years. Also people don't have any money so it wasn't a very busy year. It isn't enough to make a living. But it works that way with everything here, we're leading half a life which means it takes eight years to finish college.'

His hands rest on his knees and he waits for my reaction, but I behave as if I want him to continue and he does.

'I'll tell you something probably nobody has told you. During the past four years ninety per cent of the Palestinian Christians who graduated from foreign universities haven't come back. I am not exaggerating, ninety per cent. What a national catastrophe.' (Later others, including the reliable Bernard Sabella, confirm this without attaching an exact figure to it.)

I thank him for his revealing statement and I ask about how this reduced existence has affected the way he and his family live.

'Easy, very easy. We've cut down on both the quality and quantity of food. Meat is a rare happening nowadays and we eat eggs one day a week, nothing else but eggs. Forget about taking my kids to a picnic or the beach, things like that are completely out of the question. I can't afford it. I don't know what a holiday is. We, people in my position, don't know who to complain to, who to turn to. Who's responsible for us? The Israelis would rather see us leave, or die. Our leaders, who're our leaders and where are they? The church? The church isn't helping with anything, and the church should try to help people with schooling and housing. Even when it comes to the outside world, we don't know what is happening to us. Some people say the EEC has sent money to help us. Where the devil is it?'

I decide to stay close to the emigration story. 'I know you haven't decided to emigrate, but you're considering it. Is there anything else you can tell me as to why you're considering leaving?'

'Because there is no hope here. What exists here is a state of siege. With time this may come to be seen as one of the longest sieges in history, it's been on since '67. Think of it, that's what the Israeli occupation has created and we're in it and like all people under siege our situation gets worse with time.'

'What about the Islamic fundamentalists? Have they contributed to the state of siege?'

'Not that I am aware of, but things are so bad we don't feel little irritations. The big problem is the Israeli occupation and the consequent economic situation. If there is a Muslim problem, and I mean if, then it is so far behind it doesn't show.'

'If you have messages to the various governments and groups in the world who're concerned with your affairs, what would they be?'

'To the churches outside, in the West, I'd say feel with us. Learn how I live, hear the shooting directed at us and hear the cries of the people. Our children are so traumatized they can't absorb education any more. Help us, please.

'To the leaders of our local churches I'd say help me if you want me to stay. I can't do it alone.

'My message to the outside world is a simple one. Christians, Muslims and Jews are all human beings, please help us.'

'What about the PLO, any messages to the PLO?'

'They can't help me, they need help themselves.'

The host and I roar with uncontrolled laughter and Maurice, realizing the significance of what he's said, joins in. He leans forward to make a final statement.

'Look, I stay here because I belong here, because this is my country. But this feeling is getting weaker all the time. Do you realize that all the people in their twenties are gone? My God, my God.'

Maurice ends by telling how genuinely touched he is by my interest in what he has to say. He shakes my hand, nods and walks out of the house leaving me consumed by a strange feeling of helplessness. I walk down the street to catch a taxi back to Jerusalem. An Israeli patrol stops me and asks for my identity papers and I give them my passport. They ask me what I was doing there and I tell them that I was visiting a friend. 'A Christian gentleman by the name of Maurice Abdallah Nassar.'

Not knowing what to do, and viewing attempts to stop emigration as a prolongation of human suffering are things common to most people and organizations directly or indirectly concerned with the problems of the Palestinian Christians. While I am inclined to agree that the local and outside churches can be blamed for not trying to do more, solving the problem requires drastic changes in many conditions on the ground which are beyond their resources and ability. Unfortunately, solutions to the problems of Israeli occupation and the consequent problems of Islamic fundamentalism and lack of economic opportunity are not in sight and Rami Meo's decision to leave and Nassar's painful decision to stay are two sides of a loaded coin.

A HOUSE DIVIDED

ISLAM INFLAMED

The Protestant Christian lawyer Jonathan Khuttab glances into the enclosed garden of the American Colony Hotel looking for someone and sees me sitting in a far corner. He waves at me and I wave back. Jonathan is a new acquaintance but he has been extremely helpful in giving me the names of people who can help me with my project. Jonathan is also a well-known defender in the Israeli law courts of *intifada* children.

The man sitting with me notices the friendliness of my salutation and asks me whether I know Jonathan well. My true answer is that I've just met him, but that he has been generous with his time and counsel. My friend and colleague (the man is a well-known journalist) frowns on my use of complimentary adjectives. 'He's a pig, you know. He's the worst kind of Christian bigot, the type who wants to take things back to the twenties and thirties when the Christians were the only educated people here and spoke for an ignorant Muslim population. They dealt with the world on our behalf then, and they want to do it again.'

I am utterly stunned, by the content of the statement and by the vehemence with which it is delivered. And of course there is the source of the comment to consider, the supposedly educated man, a formulator of local opinion and one who thinks he is educating me in the nuances of the local conditions including inter-faith relationships.

I swallow hard and try not to make an issue out of the

unacceptable accusation. 'Tell me more about that. What was happening in the twenties and thirties? I thought we Palestinians had no sectarian problem?'

'Who told you that? We did and we still do. It isn't like Lebanon, it's different. In Lebanon the conflict is over who runs the country, but here the Christians are too few to compete for that. So they can't run the country directly, but they try to do it indirectly, by controlling money and commerce which depend on our contacts with the outside world. In a way what they're trying to do isn't very different from what the Christians in Lebanon are trying to do: they're after control.'

'By saying they're trying to go back to the twenties and thirties are you saying that they controlled things then?'

'Yes, of course they did, very much so. If you looked at a list of who represented foreign companies, European and American organizations and the banks then you will see that they were all Christians. Even aid programmes to the Palestinians after the First World War and the 1936 rebellion were controlled by them, and they always favoured their own people. They controlled a lot of the wealth of the land, a disproportionate amount of it.'

'But you said it's because they were educated. Isn't it normal for educated people to make more money than the rest?'

'Yes, I can't deny that. But things have changed and we're educated now and they still want to deputise for us in our relations with the outside world. I mean we're dependent on the outside world for our livelihood once again, and they want to play the role of middleman between the world and the Muslims. Why should they? Jonathan is so prejudiced against the Muslims; he deals only with Christians. I am surprised you're defending him and defending what they're doing.'

'I'm hardly defending him. I hardly know the man, though everything I've seen is good. I'm surprised there is such a feeling against our Christian brothers.'

The man doesn't answer me; he falls into angry silence.

A few days after this incident, on a Friday, I decide to use the
quiet of the Muslim sabbath to visit Aunt Mariam in
Bethany. I arrive in the village at 11.30 in the morning and
find that she has gone to Jerusalem to pray at Al-Asqa
Mosque (part of the huge religious compound which includes
the Dome of the Rock). I am extremely surprised that
Mariam is making the effort. I had been aware of her
growing adherence to Muslim observances and that she now
performs her prayers five times a day, but I had no idea that
her religious feelings were strong enough to impel her to
make the trip to Jerusalem on a mercilessly hot day.

I turn down an invitation from a cousin to wait for Mariam
at his place and decide to visit Al-Uzzeir Mosque in Bethany
(Al-Uzzeir means Lazarus and he is also holy to Muslims).
On my way to the mosque the electronically aided loud-
speaker is bellowing a loud call to prayer which is echoing
throughout the surrounding hills and it superimposes itself on
all else.

The situation at the mosque completes the picture for me,
it adds to the attack on Jonathan and Mariam's absence. The
mosque is full and there is an overflow on to the street and
people continue to come and automatically fall in line and
begin to pray. When the noon prayer is finally over I notice
that the participants belong to all age groups. Among them
are teenagers in jeans, elderly men in traditional dress and
middle-aged men with the square beards worn by Muslim
fundamentalists. This all-age participation in Friday prayers
is new to me; when I was a child in Bethany only old people
attended Friday prayers, and a small number of them at that.
Indeed, Friday prayer attendees were the subject of
irreverent though innocent jokes. I walk back to Mariam's
place in the company of a distant cousin, an eighteen-year-
old who had participated in the prayers. 'Is the mosque full
like this every Friday?'

'Oh yes. Everybody prays now; people are much more
religious than they used to be, much more. It's stress; people
are always much more religious under conditions of stress.'

'But young people like yourself, are you feeling the stress
also?'

'Yes, yes. Time was when old people assumed responsibility for things, but this has changed as well. We can't have one thing and not the other, after all the *intifada* is a young people's revolt.'

'Is it strictly a religious matter or is there a political aspect to the return to religion?'

'No, it's mostly religious. There are Islamic political groups, but most of the people who worship are not political. People have returned to religion because they don't have anything else. I mean they no longer believe the lies of the politicians and others and the only truth is in the Qur'an.'

My cousin has nothing new to impart and I sit in Mariam's garden and wait for her until she returns. Having made the pilgrimage to Mecca six years ago, she's now respectfully addressed as Hajja. She arrives wearing the Palestinian villager's equivalent of her Sunday best, kisses me both cheeks and continues to mumble something Qur'anic.

'*Ma'boula, ya Hajja*' (May Allah accept, Hajja).

'Thank you, thank you, it's the least one can do. It's a little hot, but I just like praying at Al-Aqsa and I try to go as often as I can. The place was packed, you could hardly move. But it was lovely praying with so many people; prayer with groups is a blessing, the prophet said. Oh, I do feel so much better. Sit down on that couch, it's more comfortable. I'll make you some coffee.'

I have a difficult time convincing the Hajja I don't need lunch and we talk about religion and her feelings on the subject.

'Yes, I've been going to the Al-Aqsa for a few years now, almost regularly. It feels much better praying with thousands and thousands of people, and these are difficult times. Your uncle, Allah bless his soul, never prayed except on the occasions of the big holidays, the Eid and the Feast of Sacrifice. He did it as a ceremony, because he was the mayor and everybody expected him to be there, but he wasn't serious about it. Most people were like him in the past, but that's changed: people are genuinely religious now. You know I don't think I've missed one prayer in seven years, maybe more. Your Aunt Fatmeh and the rest are praying as well, and she made the pilgrimage.'

'So the number of people who go to pray and who're making the pilgrimage has increased, has it?'

'Yes, yes, all these things have increased. People need religion now, the Qu'ran is the only source of help we have, Allah is our only protector.'

'Let me ask you something, two things. How do you feel about the Israeli plans to demolish the Dome of the Rock and the Aqsa Mosque and build the Third Temple, the Jewish holy temple?'

She lowers her head and holds the tips of her fingers together. Then, shaking her head back and forth, she answers, 'If they do that, if they touch the Dome of the Rock and the Mosque then we'll all have to go. We don't have any arms to stop them, so we'll all have to go.'

'Let's see if I understand you: are you saying that you'd all die defending the Dome of the Rock?'

'I am saying that and more; I am saying we can't allow them to do that and live.'

I look at her, petite and pretty in defiance of her age, hardly the picture of a revolutionary or a Muslim zealot, but a simple committed Muslim nevertheless, one who means what she says in a more threatening way than is conveyed by the bellicose words of those accustomed to uttering them.

'I am going to ask you another question about something which has happened here, in Bethany. There are a few Christian families who live here now, and that's relatively new. How do you feel about that, about the Christian presence in Bethany?'

'The monasteries and churches have always been here, long before my time. So you're talking about the people, Christian residents. There are people who object to their presence, but I am not one of those people. I have seen nothing but good from them, and most of them are very clean and well-brought up; but there are others who object.'

'Why do the others object?'

'Things are changing in many ways. For example, women's dress is more modest and more Islamic and some people think the Christians exert an influence against that. Then there is the business of the more open relationships between youngsters of different sexes, and people object to that as well and think it is infectious. It's very difficult for me to pinpoint it, but it has to do with people becoming more religious.'

Later the same day, my cousin Khalil, Mariam's son, articulates what his mother failed to explain. 'Said, when my father encouraged the Christians to move to Bethany, he did it because they were more modern, which meant more Western. Indeed they were, and their ways influenced ours in what we considered a very healthy way. What has happened since, with the Islamic resurgence, is that nobody wants to emulate the West, in other words what the Christians have to offer is now rejected.'

'But Khalil, how serious is it, is there trouble?'

'No, no, nothing of the sort, but perhaps it's on the way. I am not the man to talk about this. I am all for their presence here for the original reason and I think they've been an excellent influence on this community and long may it continue. This is not to pretend that others don't think differently, because they do. There is a feeling among some groups that it is the Muslims who're under heavy pressure from the Israelis, they equate the Christians' relative wellbeing with something else, with being protected from the pressures which exist. This is simply not correct.'

I decide that the next step is to determine how the situation is felt, seen and perceived by the Christians. I make notes to myself to include open, pointed questions on the subject during my forthcoming meeting with Roman Catholic Patriarch Michel Sabbah. The Roman Catholic Patriarchy is a massive old building just inside Jerusalem's Jaffa Gate. One can reach it via a narrow road full of pedestrian traffic, a mixture of tourists and local people who live in some of the attractive old houses of the city. Taxis have difficulty in negotiating the narrow street and I leave the one taking me to my appointment to walk the last fifty yards.

A man is shouting at the passers by, loudly and in an irritating way but there is no serious menace in his voice.

People continue on their way without paying much attention to what he is doing, and I can't decipher it until I am close to him. He is in his middle years, gesturing a bit wildly but what he is saying is more of a request than a demand.

'Cover your hair, sisters, it is a sin to have your hair exposed. You should obey the words of the prophet and wear modest dress. Those who do not will pay for it on the day of judgement.' I watch the man without exposing myself to the possibility of offending him. He doesn't linger there but moves on repeating his religious howls. I find the call, which is almost an incitement, to people to observe Muslim ways of dress and behaviour disturbingly revealing.

The man is obviously a bit of zealot who can't control his feelings, perhaps a harmless one to whom the people of the neighbourhood are accustomed, but capable of odd street showmanship nevertheless. The people who hear him are determined to ignore him to the extent of pretending he isn't there, and they include a number of Christian religious people and – and this is provoking his exhortation – a number of Christian ladies in Western dress.

The question is whether ignoring the man is enough. The challenge he represents is dramatized by the fact that it is taking place in front of the Roman Catholic Patriarchy, it is as if he's questioning the Patriarchy's right to provide guidance to its followers and the Christians who listen to him are obviously afraid. Perhaps much more telling is the fact that the Muslims who listen to him are too afraid to ask him to stop, let alone admonish him for interfering in the way of life of their Christian brothers. If we view the behaviour of the man as particularly strange in the Middle East, where men don't talk to women in the streets, and an extreme expression of the preoccupations of this time, then this simple challenge is very serious indeed.

The Patriarch's secretary ushers me into a small room full of low, cushioned chairs and crucifixes. Statues of the Virgin Mary are everywhere, but I have no chance to look at them. The Patriarch is there in his official garb, a smallish man who holds his hands together reverently and responds to my nod with a request for me to sit down. Coffee is ordered, and we start the interview after I thank him for seeing me at such short notice. Forty-five minutes later we're in the middle of a discussion about Muslim–Christian relations and the effects of the growing Muslim fundamentalist movement.

'It is a very sad situation. Israeli political suppression created Islamic fundamentalism, an extreme response to extreme political pressure. After all the Israeli attitude is an expression of religion so it is no surprise that the response to it is the same.'

'Are there any clear manifestations of this extreme Muslim attitude that you allude to?'

'Yes, we have a new organization here called the Army of Muhammad. It's a secret group, and we don't know much about it beyond the fact that it started in Jordan. But everything we hear about it suggests that its members are very uncompromising and that they want a purely religious state which leaves little room for other people and other opinions; and whether they admit it or not that would affect the Christians. To give you an idea: in Jordan some of them have just gone on trial for conspiring to overthrow the government through violent means.'

'Have they done anything here? Are there any signs of Muslim militancy here?'

His hands are entwined and his voice is gentle with some pain in it. 'Yes, there have been. The Islamic students in Bethlehem University demanded a room in which to conduct Muslim prayer. We welcome the idea of anybody praying, but providing them with much needed space did create a problem, and it was a challenge to the administration.'

The Patriarch refrains from mentioning the obvious fact that Bethlehem was and is Vatican sponsored. It is a Christian university which has never discriminated against anyone and students are admitted on the basis of merit. The demand of a Muslim prayer room is a deliberate strike against the university's Christian identity, perhaps a prelude to challenging it and eventually changing it.

'What about violent acts against the Christians? Have you had any of them?'

'Unhappily yes, very unhappily yes. There have been a

number of incidents involving Christian graveyards; they have been desecrated, and there were writings on tomb stones which I do not care to repeat. In the Selesian Nunnery in Bethlehem the statue of the Virgin Mary was destroyed, right in the small inside garden. My own car and those belonging to others were torched while we attended a meeting of religious leaders and Christian notables in Bethlehem last year. There have been several incidents where the Crescent has been raised from church towers during the night.

'Both sides, the Muslim side and the Christian side must be careful or things will get out of hand; both sides must understand that they're under pressure and pressure creates an atmosphere of unreason and we cannot allow that to happen.'

'What are you doing to stop this? Is there anything you're doing with the Muslim religious leadership?'

'Our relations with the traditional leadership of our Muslim brothers are very good; we're in constant contact with them and they totally disapprove of all acts of this nature. That is not where the problem is, the problem is with young people who're frustrated because the *intifada* hasn't yielded the desired results, and they're turning to extremism.

'And do not forget that the Israelis would like to see the problem between the two sides flourish. Every time there is the smallest incident they play it up, and on one occasion, on 23 December 1990, Israeli Radio criticized the Christians for not responding to Muslim intransigence. Yes, they try to foment trouble whenever they can.'

'What about the Christians as a group, have you done anything to respond to the realities of the new situation?'

'Yes, there is the Council of Churches and we consult among ourselves regarding our common problems. It is a very sad situation with so many pressures descending upon us.'

Our conversation continues for sometime, but it deals with the overall situation and patriarch Sabbah concludes with the usual appeal to the West 'to understand the truth of what is happening in the Holy Land'. In view of consistent reports that Patriarch Sabbah had complained to Israeli groups about Muslim behaviour, I have no idea what truth he is talking about.

My next meeting is in Bethlehem, with Jiryes Said Khoury, the director of Al-Liqa Centre for Religious Study in the Holy Land. A rabid Palestinian nationalist with strong views on everything, Dr Khoury denies the existence of a problem with Muslim fundamentalists and rages against Israel ('it is trying to divide us, it is racial in origin'), religious leadership ('we can't afford a Muslim–Christian gap'), advocates of assumption of local leadership of overall Palestinian power ('there's only one PLO and we follow it') and even the Mormons ('they aren't Christians, they're neo-colonialists'). All attempts to get him to offer an opinion on the problems between the Muslims and Christians are buried in a sea of verbal accusations which are not substantiated and although extremely informative overall have little to do with the immediate question. In reality Khoury's loud dissertations and accusations are a diplomatic smokescreen.

On my way back to Jerusalem I leaf through some of the pieces of literature the irrepressible Doctor Khoury generously gave to me. One of the pamphlets of his organization claims that one of the purposes of Al-Liqa Centre is to promote Christian–Muslim dialogue and it goes further to ask whether Islamic fundamentalism frightens the Christians but provides no answer. What the publication states and omits and what the outspoken Dr Khoury refuses to address are answers unto themselves.

The refusal to admit that Islamic fundamentalism has affected the traditional harmony of Muslim-Christian relations and that it poses a present or prospective threat to the Christian way of life is a prevalent attitude among many Christians. Among religious leaders, Bishop Samir Kafity of the Anglican Church provides a typical answer. 'Nonsense, we have no problem with our Muslim brothers. On the contrary, we stand united in the face of a common threat and a common enemy.' Zhogbi Zhogbi of the Middle East

Council of Churches uses words which are less guarded. 'I am Arab, Palestinian and Christian in that order. Any attempt to change this order of loyalty is disloyalty itself.' But, during the same meeting which witnessed this unequivocal statement of identity, his colleague, Roscoe Passadente, told me about leaflets objecting to Sunday closures being distributed in Christian schools and left it for me to conclude that the pamphleteers wanted a Muslim Friday school closure.

I am convinced that the problem exists; I can feel it in the way people talk about it, even when they deny its existence, and I can hear it in the unnatural references used by both Muslims and Christians. I tell myself that I am chasing a crooked shadow and that what I see with my own eyes and hear from innocents like my Aunt Mariam and the courageous statements of Patriarch Sabbah are closer to the truth.

Finally I am with someone who will discuss the problem openly, provided his identity is withheld and I accept the condition of anonymity and the further condition that some minor facts will be altered to guard against the speaker's identification. The precautionary steps required speak of a fear which is new to the situation under investigation.

He is young, in his early thirties, and the father of two children. He has been teaching at college level but has given that up to devote himself to his family business. A worldly, modern person with an admitted streak of hedonism, he claims that calling things by their proper names 'is a problem the Arabs must overcome. If I choose to admit that a problem exists, it isn't because I like the idea but because it is there and the only way to solve it is to make this admission and proceed to try to solve the problem in a sensible way.' It is a proposition with which I have no quarrel and I obtain his agreement to take the whole issue from beginning to end.

'I take it you are in agreement that there is a problem between the Christians and the Muslims of the Holy Land brought about by the emergence of a new militant Muslim fundamentalist movement.'

He smiles at my repetition of his words. 'Yes, there is a problem, and it is a problem which is growing worse with time and needs to be admitted. Without admitting it's there we can't solve it; not that solving it is predictable or is going to be easy.'

'Do you mind giving your assessment of what the problem is.'

'I like the way you made that statement. We do need to identify what the problem is before we talk about it. The problem is the total breakdown of the social order and the reversion to tribalism. The success of the *intifada* has led to a breakdown in law and order and in return this has led to tribalism, a narrower view of things. Within that the Muslims have gone back to the Muslim tribe, a larger, less open group than the Palestinian whole, and that group wants to protect itself against everything, even the Christians who don't belong to it.'

'This is understandable to me, but what does it mean in everyday relations between Christians and Muslims?'

The man smiles benignly. 'Yes, we must reduce it to examples in order to understand it. Right, I am a Christian and a Catholic and six years ago I moved to your home town of Bethany and lived there for a year. While I was there somebody broke into our house and stole the television set and a few other things. I went to the mayor – your cousin I believe – and lodged the usual complaint. I had the feeling that everybody in Bethany knew who the perpetrator of the crime was, but the mayor did nothing about it. I was a Christian and an outsider and he wasn't about to offend his Muslim constituency to please me. This is an example of tribalism; had it been a member of his family against the Muslim community he would have supported his cousin and his family.'

'What did this have to do with relations between the Muslims and the Christians?'

'Everything. What Hammas and the other Islamic fundamentalist movements are saying is that the national identity, Palestinianism, has failed. They've been saying that they're Palestinian-Arabs or Arab-Palestinians for ages and it hasn't produced anything. Now they want to say that they're Muslims.'

'Tell me more of how his shows itself in everyday life.'

'I think you're having problems with my point of view. Let's look at it differently, let's take into consideration another aspect of the problem between Muslims and Christians. I think it's fair to say that most Muslims blame the West for all or part of the Arab defeat in Palestine. As a result they don't like the West. Simultaneously, the church, the local Christian churches here, equates progress with modernization with Westernization; they haven't heard about what Japan did in Manchuria. Indirectly, anybody who's against Westernization is against the West and automatically becomes anti-church which means anti-Christian. In other words, the Christians are resented because they belong to the West which is against the Arabs and caused their defeat.'

'Again, how does this show itself in everyday life?'

'Very simply, the Muslim clergy are all Palestinians, but the Christian clergy come from all over the world and until recently the heads of the churches were non-Arabs. It is a question of whether you can be a loyal Arab and Christian at the same time, or whether local Christian loyalty to the church means loyalty to the West.'

'And that's held against the Christians?'

'Yes, rightly, the Christian churches here are criminal, they're beholden to outsiders, and I belong to one. They have to make up their mind whether to belong to Rome or Constantinople or whether their job is to serve the people here. If they belong to the people then they should do what the church in South America has done, rebel.'

'But surely that's not why Islamic fundamentalists are adopting anti-Christian behaviour?'

'Islamic fundamentalism is an attempt at changing the nature of the confrontation with the West. They're saying it is a religious rather than a nationalistic confrontation, the whole Muslim world is involved, over one billion of them.'

'But how does anti-Christian feeling show itself here?'

'I think that's what you wanted to hear from the start. They're trying to get the Christians to renounce their connections with the West and go East. So Christians working with Western people are frowned upon; the visits of religious figures like the Pope are not appreciated, the Christian role of being the link between the two sides is no longer appreciated; and Christian organizations which are Western in origin are suspected of fronting for other anti-Arab groups.

'Let me give you concrete examples. Nobody wants a YMCA here because it's originally American. Its Christian directors are accused of being in the pay of the CIA. This accusation is also levelled against the directors of the YWCA and the Middle East Council of Churches. Christians leaders visiting the Holy Land never speak of our suffering without speaking of the suffering of the Jews and that automatically makes them – and the people who follow them – suspect. You don't see a Muslim cleric talking about the suffering of the Jews. Most of the employees of the UN and the various Western consulates are Christians and that makes them suspect in the eyes of their Muslim compatriots. What all this has produced are angry Muslims who resent everything Christian and what they're seeing amounts to a threat: either belong or leave.'

I control my desire to defend the accused, several of whom are known to me as committed humanitarians and loyal Palestinians. 'And they have desecrated Christian graveyards and destroyed statues of the Virgin Mary and raised the Crescent on top of church towers – is that what they've done?'

'Yes, they have, and there have been incidents of them being disrespectful to nuns and priests and of forcing Christian shops to shut on Friday and of requesting that the ringing of church bells be stopped and so on. And it will get worse.'

To say it was the most difficult interview I've ever conducted would be an exaggeration, but it was very close to it. My interviewee was determined to make the philosophical point that the anti-Christian Islamic fundamentalist position is nothing more than a reaction to the Christian churches' identification with a perfidious West which is against the Arabs. But in fairness to him, no less than six other people held the same strong view, and some, like Professor Jad Izhaq and social worker Rifaat Audeh, went as far as to accuse the Christian church as a whole of wilfull criminal activity against its own people.

The second man I grant anonymity is an eighty-one-year-old priest with a proud record of resistance to Israeli rule. He's also extremely popular in the mixed Muslim–Christian community where he lives.

'Father, are you telling me that there is anti-Christian feeling in this community?'

'Yes, and it is growing stronger – it's the worst I've known it for sixty years, for all the time I've been here.'

'This is a mixed community, how does it show itself?'

'The Muslim community is becoming much more religious, so much more than before. I think Israeli pressure has something to do with it, or general stress which makes people turn religious. I don't know, but they are, and for the first time ever this is also true of the very young people and this is where the danger lies. There is no problem with being religious, as a priest I have to accept that, but there is a problem with negative religion and that's what we've got in this case. The Christians are becoming religious as well, but it doesn't show as much – Islam is an outward religion in that it shows itself.'

'How does the division between Muslims and Christians express itself, are you able to provide me with examples?'

'Unfortunately yes. There were some graffiti on the outside walls around the church and they weren't very nice. And there was one incident which could have turned nasty, a group of tourists passed in front of the mosque as people were breaking from prayer, and that too wasn't very nice. There was that ugly case of the female missionary in Bethlehem who was murdered by a Muslim fundamentalist [he couldn't provide me with more information]; it sent shivers down the spine of the Christian community. I am told there are a number of cases where Christian children have to recite the Qur'an in school and so on.'

'Father, I appreciate your candour, do tell me if you really feel the pressure.'

'Oh yes, it's in the atmosphere, people aren't as relaxed about inter-faith relations as they used to be. Whatever they do has a ring of trying too hard about it. I mean think of poor Hannan Ashrawi [the Palestinian spokeswoman at the Peace Conference]. They released pamphlets attacking her, said that she's unacceptable as a Christian and a woman. Can you believe that, after all she's done. What do you think action like this does to the Christian community? It frightens them, it widens the divide separating them from the Muslims, it's very bad.'

'And this is all new?'

'Yes, relations were good between the two sides until a few years ago and now . . .'

'And they're getting worse?'

'Yes, it takes something very small to poison the atmosphere between the two sides and so much work to undo the damage. The important thing is the lack of trust.'

The pieces of the mosaic are adding up to the big picture; all I need are the representative thoughts of a Muslim fundamentalist. I reach one of them through the good offices of cousin Fathi and he consents to see me. He is exactly what I want, a middle-rank operative whose opinions incorporate both the leadership and street thinking of the movement.

The man is wearing a black beard and his head is covered with a white Muslim cap. He is in his thirties and he sits cross-legged with prayer beads in his hand. He confirms that he is a graduate of one of Jerusalem's better known high schools and that he speaks English – but would rather not do so. He is married and the father of four children. He became a fundamentalist after years as a member of Fateh, the Arafat-led PLO group, and after deciding that 'religion is the only way'.

'Brother Muhammad, what are the aims of the organization to which you belong?'

He smiles benignly while he clicks his beads. 'Our aims are

not a secret. Foremost among them is to defeat our Israeli enemy. And, to us, the only way to defeat this enemy is through Islam, through commitment to religion and its commands.'

'Is it possible for you to be more specific? I mean what is your programme of action against the Israeli enemy?'

The smile is much bigger and he is self-satisfyingly patronizing. 'Surely, Brother Said, you do not expect me to reveal our programme of action to you to publish to the rest of the world.'

'No, I don't expect that, but can we get beyond the usual generalities – perhaps I can ask some small questions.'

'Go ahead.'

'Do you advocate the use of violence against Israel?'

'They use violence against us. We're defending ourselves, our country and our property.'

'Do you advocate unity among Muslims?'

'Yes, we believe that there is strength in unity.'

'Do you advocate political unity among the Muslim countries?'

'If their people support such unity then we're all for it.'

I tire of this approach and decide to concentrate on the subject matter concerning me. 'What kind of a state, what government would you have here, if you had your way?'

'I am sure you mean if it is the wish of the people. We would have a Muslim Government which would subscribe to the teachings of the Qur'an.'

'And would you expect everybody to follow those teachings?'

'If they become the law of the land, then everybody would have to obey the law.'

'But what happens if these laws interfere with the religion of other people, the Christians for example?'

'Our Christian brothers have never had anything to worry about, the Christians have lived safely under the Muslims for centuries.'

'Forgive me, but what I am after is very simple. What if the laws enacted by a Muslim state infringe, place constraints, on the Christian way of life?'

'The law is the law, everybody would have to obey it.'

'Yes, but what if the law requires women to cover their hair, and what if the law requires people not to work on Friday and what if the law requires religious education in schools? Would you force the Christians to obey this law when their religion says otherwise?'

'Islamic laws protect the rights of the individual and we do not discriminate. We have never discriminated against our Christian brothers, never.'

'What about things like the attacks on Christian graveyards and the destruction of the statue of the Virgin Mary? These happened, and they're attributed to some of your followers. Tell me what you think of them?'

'I don't believe they happened, and if they happened then they were not carried out by our followers. Islam has clear commands against the desecration of graves and such action is totally prohibited. And the Virgin Mary is the only woman in the Qur'an and she is revered by us at the mother of the prophet Jesus who is most holy to us.'

'So you don't believe that anything you advocate is against or indirectly endangers the welfare of the Christian community in the Holy Land?'

'Most certainly not. Our Christian brothers are just that, our revered Christian brothers. What we advocate is very simple: the use of all available means to defeat our Zionist enemies and their supporters. The declaration of a permanent state of Jihad until this aim is achieved.'

'One last question: who according to you, are those who support the Zionist enemy?'

'Western governments and organizations.'

'Churches?'

'Some of them.'

The answer is not illusive, I tell myself as I walk out of the religious zealot's humble abode, the answer was given to me several times but I refused to accept it because I thought it was more complicated. The natural divide between Islam and Christianity has widened. Islam is becoming more militant at a time when the Christians of the Holy Land are becoming more moderate. Islam's militancy means an anti-West stand and the Christian moderation means closer identification with the newly moderate PLO and closer ties to the West. The conflict is built in, they're going in two different directions and the further along they go the worse things are going to get.

THE CHRISTIANS AGAINST
THEMSELVES

It is early in the evening and I am in my hotel room. I tire of the depressing chore of transcribing and expanding my notes of the day and turn to the *Jerusalem Post* for a change of mood. As usual the newspaper is full of stories about children getting arrested, wounded and killed; trees being uprooted; international, religious and humanitarian study groups confirming unhappy old stories and various members of the Israeli cabinet and local Arab leaders repeating themselves. On page three of the same issue of the *Post* is a totally Christian story, a reminder that the Christian problem has its own separate unhappy identity.

The *Post*'s story says that the International Christian Embassy plans to hold its twelfth Feast of the Tabernacles World Gathering next week. Four thousand people from seventy-five countries are expected to attend and 'the participants represent tens of millions of pro-Israel Christians in their home countries.' Among the events of the forthcoming conference is a solidarity march through Jerusalem.

I circle the story of the Christian Embassy, wonder why nobody has told me about the group and make notes for myself to inquire about its activities. The question of how a Christian group sees fit to support Israel at a time when their co-religionists are subjected to untold economic hardships, when their land is being expropriated and their children imprisoned and tortured, and when their Christian way of life is threatened and subordinated to a larger more inclusive one. To me the overriding question is whether Christian support for Israel as exemplified by the Christian Embassy is indeed a betrayal of the local community or whether there is no betrayal whatsoever because it is the local community which is out of step with an overall picture of Christian support for Israel.

The following morning, my learned friend Bernard Sabella explains the position of the Christian Embassy to me. 'They are Zionist Christians, mostly evangelist groups; in this case the Embassy is a US-Dutch group. They see Israel as the prelude to the Second Coming and support it vigorously. But the business of the second coming and the blind support for Israel is not the position of the mainline churches, the Catholics, Greek Orthodox, Anglicans and others. I don't know what conclusion you're trying to draw, but the Christian community here isn't out of step with the rest of the world's Christians and their complaint about betrayal is legitimate.'

I am a great admirer of Bernard Sabella, but I don't find his answer totally convincing. The source of my unease is the numbers staring me in the eye, a Christian group which is able to gather 4,000 (in April 1988 they managed 5,000) Christian supporters of Israel at a time is not to be dismissed as an aberration. The spokesman for the Christian Embassy, a Dutchman by the name of Jan Willem Van der Hoeven, adds to my gnawing unease by telling me that they have the support of forty million US Bible-belt Christians. I decide to take the problem to the various authorities and consultants I use to get answers to difficult questions like this.

My first meeting is with David Newhouse, the already-mentioned authority on the subject of Christianity in the Holy Land. A South African who has converted to Catholicism from Judaism, David got his Ph.D. in divinity from the Hebrew University and the subject of his thesis was the Christian Churches of the Holy Land. He lives in the Convent of the Sisters of St Joseph in Prophets' Street. He is thirty-two, sandalled and dressed in the manner of a 1960s hippy, and refreshingly outspoken.

'David, who are the members of the Christian Embassy, they sound like a bunch of nuts, but they sound big and influential . . . tell me.'

David adjusts his glasses and smiles. 'They're hardly a bunch of nuts, this is a very serious piece of business. They do represent millions of people, make no mistake about that. Your best bet is to read Marcel Dubois, yes Marcel is the man to meet and read. He is a Dominican father, the head of the Philosophy Department of the Hebrew University. Marcel believes that the only true Christians are the believers in the Second Coming and the believers in the Second Coming are people who believe that Israel is a prelude to it.'

'So, we have a Dominican father who supports this theory?'

'Yes, very strongly, very, very strongly indeed. It isn't only people like Marcel, but there are many others. So many the Israeli authorities go far enough to accept the evangelists and the rest of the believers in the Second Coming as the true Christians. They certainly treat the head of the Embassy that way and provide him with semi-diplomatic treatment.'

'That's what I can't get straight. Does Christian support for Israel follow clear lines, and do the mainline churches support the local Christians against Israel, or how does it divide?'

'For the most part the mainline churches do support the local Christians, but this support is far from being universal and there is a big question as to the quality of this support. But Christian support is divided; Christianity is like the PLO, it's an umbrella organization, and it goes in different directions. For example the nuns here, the Sisters of St Joseph, support the State of Israel and so do the Sisters of Jesus for that matter. Both are Catholic groups and Marcel is a Catholic, at least nobody has excommunicated him yet.'

There is much to laugh about in what David says and he is obviously enjoying the business of educating me in the twists and turns of inter-church and inter-Christian relations. 'Look, Said, you're taking this business of Christian support

for Israel as a betrayal of the local Christians too much to
heart. The Christian churches' presence in the Holy Land
isn't for the purpose of helping the local people, it has never
been for the local people and therefore their failure to
provide political support can't be seen as betrayal. Start from
there, yes that's a good point to start, by questioning the
reason for the presence of the various churches in the Holy
Land and through that you'll see the whole relationship and
structure and many things will become clear to you. The
churches are here to be in Jerusalem, not to help the locals. I
had better equip you for this. Come with me and I will give
you something to read on the subject.'

The publications David gives me prove helpful, but only in
an academic, cerebral way. They do not deal with the area of
my primary concern: the human face of the tragedy of the
Christians of the Holy Land. They do, however, provide an
acceptable outline of the problems Christians have among
themselves in the following four ways:

The Christian churches of the Holy Land (Roman
Catholic, Greek Orthodox, Anglican, Copts, Greek
Catholics, Armenian and others) are divided by ideological
and other differences and the resulting divisions weaken
the Christian presence in the Holy Land, substantially.

There are serious differences between most of the local
churches and their mother churches over the limited
financial, spiritual and political support provided by the
latter to alleviate the conditions of misery of their
co-religionists.

There is a severe crisis of confidence between the local
Christian faithful and their churches. Many local Christians
accuse their churches of obeying the dictats of an
insensitive outside church at the expense of the interests of
the local community.

The Christian Zionist movement has undermined the
Palestinian Christian presence in the Holy Land and its
uncritical support of Israel threatens the very existence of
local Christianity.

To an outsider, the problems dividing the local Christian churches of the Holy Land appear the stupid work of selfish negligent people who ignore the major threats to their existence and devote much time and energy to minor destructive squabbles. But the feuds between the local Christian churches look considerably different to the people who participate in them. Al-Liqa director Jiryes Said Khoury agrees with much of what David Newhouse has to say and adds that the division among the local Christian churches is lamentable. 'There's strength in numbers, but they don't understand that, nobody is willing to compromise. Every local Christian leader thinks he's the voice of Christianity in the Holy Land.'

Both Khoury and journalist Daoud Khuttab speak of the 'curse of the Holy Land' and the importance of being the leading Christian there. Khoury and his organization conduct seminars in which the participation of the heads of the various churches is required, a vain attempt to get them to address common problems. But Khuttab isn't hopeful and he likens Holy Land Christianity to 'a business which is losing customers and those who run it will do anything to add to their clientele or give the impression that they're more successful than they really are. So, each head of church goes for representing a bigger mass, even if it is a mass made of pretending to represent Christianity in the Holy Land.'

My investigation of this issue reveals that the most divisive inter-church quarrel is the historic one between the Roman Catholics and the Greek Orthodox. The way this theological argument has shown itself in the Holy Land goes back to the Crusades, when the local Greek Orthodox church sided with the Muslims against the Roman Catholics. Today, members of the local Greek Orthodox community proudly point out that one of Saladin's top generals was Issa Anam, a Greek Orthodox from Jaffa. Certainly the record of the Crusaders' atrocities against the local Christians is a long and unhappy one.

According to professors Jad Izhaq and Albert Aggezarian, the real problem between these two churches, the one which continues to influence their attitude towards each other, took root in the Middle Ages at the time of the Latin Kingdom. Then, the Latins, our present-day Roman Catholics, tried a settlement programme similar to the one being carried out by Israel today. Sadly, the Roman Catholics are still called Latins and it is a name which doesn't appeal in many quarters.

I try but fail to get straight answers to confirm or deny this simple historical perspective from either Roman Catholic Patriarch Michel Sabbah or Greek Orthodox Patriarch Theodorous. That aside, the deep wish to claim to speak for a wounded, dying local Christianity does separate the two churches. Michel Sabbah alludes to Theodorous's Greek nationality to diminish his status; it is an indirect claim that the Arabization of the leadership of the Roman Catholics makes them more qualified to speak for local Christianity. Greek Orthodox speakers counter by claiming that the Greek Orthodox are closer to the land, real Palestinians, and that the Roman Catholics are nothing but leftovers from unwanted settlers. Nobody speaks with conviction of a real common front between the two sides.

Because they have the greatest number of followers, the quarrel between the Roman Catholics and the Greek Orthodox is the one which matters most, but it is far from being the only one. Most local Christian churches register bitter complaints against Protestant aid groups because they're supposed to favour their own people and claim more of outside Protestant aid than they need or deserve. 'Look at the Anglicans,' said an angry social worker in Beit Sahur, 'they live in a state of middle-class bliss. After all, they pocket over ninety per cent of what the Protestants send to us in aid.'

Even the centuries-old problem of who stands where inside the Church of the Holy Sepulchre on Christmas Eve remains unsolved and is taken so seriously as to provoke outbursts of violence on the holy occasion. 'Yes,' sighs historian Albert Aggezarian, 'the padres really go for it; the priests of the different churches have fights right in the middle of the Church of the Holy Sepulchre. What a shameful performance; there must be a better solution.'

Inter-faith marriages are still known to cause considerable problems and a Roman Catholic female university professor told me the story of her marriage to a non-Catholic then retracted the story and trusted me not to report it. The priests of certain churches, particularly the Roman Catholics, refuse to administer to those who marry outsiders. As a Christian worker for the local Red Cross observed, 'It's the same old story, to the Roman Catholics you aren't Christian unless you're Roman Catholic and they would rather than Christianity disappear altogether than accept the ways of fellow Christians.'

The place where the conflict between the various Christian churches shows most is in the schools they sponsor and control. In a part of the world where the hunger for education is one of the few signs of hope, and public education is inadequate, most of the good schools are church-controlled. The Catholics claim that the Anglicans exclude them from their schools and would rather admit Muslims. The Anglicans scoff at the quality of education in Roman Catholic schools and question the need to spend so much time in religious worship. Even the Quakers who run two exemplary schools in Ramallah are accused of discriminating against the Roman Catholics.

The divisions among the local Christian churches, old, new, petty and fundamental, have gone a long way towards weakening the Christian presence. There are no signs that wisdom is about to prevail, not while church leaders accuse each other of being gold smugglers and others scoffingly allude to the lavish lifestyle of their counterparts. Meetings between heads of the churches, even the creation of a Council of Churches, produce nothing; the participants tend to address themselves to small immediate problems and the overriding problem of things like a Roman Catholic–Greek Orthodox reconciliation – even a local one – is left to their mother churches which, totally divorced from the devastation of local Israeli, Muslim fundamentalist and economic pressures, do not see the need to work for a common good.

The second inter-church conflict is the less clear-cut one between the local churches of the Holy Land and their mother churches, i.e. the local Roman Catholic Church versus Rome, the Anglican Church versus Canterbury and the Greek Orthodox versus Constaninople. They begin with the existence of ideological differences, a religious response to local conditions versus universally accepted dogma, but the problems between most of the local churches and their mother churches are eventually reduced to everyday affairs which involve politics and finance.

In separate interviews, I ask the three heads of the major Christian churches (Roman Catholic, Greek Orthodox and Anglican) the same question; whether their mother church is providing them with financial and political support to cope with the pressures of their unfortunate situation. Samir Kafity, the Anglican Archbishop, has no problem providing me with an answer. He bravely accuses Canterbury of not doing enough for his church and its followers. Patriarch Michel Sabbah of the Roman Catholic church has no difficulty in blaming the West for not doing enough to help the Christians, but he refuses to blame the Vatican. Hiding behind diplomatic language, he claims that there is a general agreement between him and Rome as to 'what is possible'. Patriarch Theodorous of the Greek Orthodox church speaks through an interpreter and says that the resources available to his church are small indeed and that 'the church [used inclusively] is doing its best'.

I ask the attractively outspoken Archbishop Kafity and his equally fearless assistant, Canon Ateeq, to list the needs of the local church and its followers and to follow that with an appreciation of where Canterbury has failed to provide help.

'Our middle-class people, and most of our community is middle class, are losing their economic status. We have an emergence of poor people for the first time, and we need to support them and the rest of the local community cannot do that because they're suffering themselves. We need money for hospitals, centres for the handicapped and for schools. We need money to keep our churches open – and we've had to close one in Hebron recently. We are operating on meagre resources and doing our best, but we need help desperately and if we don't get it then our people will leave and we won't have anybody left. What we're talking about is very small indeed, but it is vital, it is needed.'

On the political front both Kafity and Ateeq are cerebrally understanding but bitter. They understand that Canterbury and the US Episcopal Bishops cannot grant them open support against the policies of the State of Israel for fear of a confrontation with the supporters of the Jewish state which would include accusations of anti-Semitism. However, they do not completely absolve their co-religionists and recite intolerable and documented cases of Israeli interference in their affairs. Ateeq in particular cannot accept the mother church's refusal to publicize the Israeli government's confiscation of church land, the restrictions applied on its schools' curriculum, the prevention of priests from reaching their churches and the occasional Israeli refusal to let them enter if they manage to get there, and the desecration of Anglican churches in Awe and Ramleh by Zionist extremists. He brings the fingers of his hands together and asks a simple question: 'What are they waiting for? Our numbers are getting smaller and smaller by the day – what are they waiting for?'

Roman Catholic Patriarch Michel Sabbah changes character when he discusses the relationship of his church to the Vatican. Until this question comes up, our discussion had centred around Israeli and Muslim pressures on his community and he had admitted to both while identifying Israel as a substantially larger and more dangerous culprit. Suddenly, when I concentrate on the subject of his relations with Rome, he resorts to a WE which leaves no doubt that he considers himself and his followers inseparable from Rome.

My persistence pays no dividend. I keep getting small answers about how Roman Catholic schools have been in the Holy Land for generations and that the same is true of hospitals and certainly of the Vatican-sponsored Bethelehem University. He answers my very specific question about possible Vatican support in the political area by referring me to papal pronouncements on the subject of the Holy Land and I know most of them to be non-committal and they represent nothing more than prayers for peace. I bring the fruitless exercise with Patriarch Michel Sabbah to an end and decide to talk to Roman Catholics in less exalted and less sensitive positions in the hope that they might feel less constrained and more able to give me straight answers.

I find Father Peter Mathes of the Papal Nuncio's office more willing to speak. As a matter of fact Father Peter is disturbingly outspoken, even to a reporter seeking to write a story or research a book.

To Father Peter, reports that the Catholic Church doesn't help or try to help are totally untrue. 'We try, and last year we gave over twelve, maybe thirteen million dollars in aid. But it all disappeared, vanished into the pockets of local Catholics. I mean some of the money was going to villages which don't even exist. We don't have much to show for the money we have spent.'

Father Peter changes direction and turns sympathetic without any prodding from me. 'How can we do the job when all we have is a hundred dollars for each local Roman Catholic and the Israelis get two thousand four hundred dollars per capita; I mean each one of them gets twenty-four times as much outside financial aid as our people do. And not only that, they wouldn't let us start a cement factory to employ people, they refuse to grant European companies licences to start small businesses and they have turned the life of the workers of the German Catholic charity Karitas into pure hell.'

'Father Peter, I am slightly confused as to where you come out on the question of Catholic aid to your local community in the Holy Land.'

'Very simply, the only way to provide aid is to do it directly, otherwise the money will disappear because the local Catholics suffer from the same social ills as the rest of the Arabs – they're corrupt. Therefore, the alternative is to provide aid through starting businesses, exporting local products and things like that. I must admit that the Israelis make this very difficult if not impossible for us to do. So very little is being done.'

'So what do you do to resolve the situation?'

'We do what we can, we give to schools, hospitals and the like. That's all.'

'Right; you have pointed out the Israeli pressures to which your local Roman Catholic community is subjected. I am sure that people like you and Patriarch Sabbah have made this situation known to the Vatican. What has the Vatican done in the political arena to help your people here?'

'The Vatican's stance regarding the problems of the Holy Land is well known; there are no secrets. We want peace in the Holy Land and we pray for a united Jerusalem which belongs to everybody and the Pope has been quite outspoken on behalf of the Palestinian refugees. This has been going on for a long time.'

'Father, if you don't mind my saying so, I think you're off on a tangent. Catholic priests have been beaten up inside the Church of the Holy Sepulchre, your church's property has been confiscated, I mean the convent of St John in the old city, you've been denied the right to open vocational centres and the intellectuals, technocrats and many of the top people of your community have been forced to emigrate. Now what have you done to help your people protect their rights?'

'The church here is helpless . . .'

'Wait, let me paraphrase the question, what has the Vatican done to help the Catholic faithful of the Holy Land in the political arena?'

'I have mentioned that we support hospitals and schools and . . .'

'And you said you give one hundred dollars to every Catholic and Jewish supporters of Israel give two thousand four hundred dollars to every Israeli. Let's go beyond that telling statistic: why hasn't the Vatican provided open political support for the local Roman Catholic community?'

'Because the Vatican cannot change its worldwide policies to accommodate the special conditions of a special community.'

'And is it – in this case – the policy of the Vatican to build bridges with the Jews worldwide and – before you answer me – does this come ahead of the welfare of your people here?'

'If that is the way you choose to see it, then fine.'

'I am sorry, father, but there is no other way I can see it. And I will go further and tell you that this places your community here in grave danger.'

He actually shrugs his shoulders. I think I am seeing things, but the good father actually shrugs his shoulders and all I can do is hope it was directed at me personally and not a sign of a lack of care towards the Roman Catholics of the Holy Land.

If the meetings with the representatives of the Anglican Church were marked by openness which amounted to a courageous declaration of independence and the meetings with the Roman Catholic leaders revealed a traditional Roman Catholic attitude of total belief in the actions of the mother church, then the meetings with Patriarch Theodorous and Father Thedoseus of the Greek Orthodox Church amount to an oriental attempt to substitute nonsense for substance.

I tire of trying to get anything out of Patriarch Theodorous. He speaks to me through an interpreter, a telling sign of how much the church cares about the welfare of the local people, and he keeps repeating that his church is poor and cannot afford the kind of aid which is needed by the people.

'But the countryside is full of monasteries which are full of priests but I see very few signs of Greek Orthodox schools or hospitals or things like that. Why is that?'

'It is because our church has very little money; we're very poor.'

'Why don't you support some schools instead of all the monasteries around?'

'The priests in the monasteries have given their lives to God and we can't deny them that.'

'Sir, if your church can't provide financial help to your local followers then what about political/diplomatic help in the international arena. What have you done about that?'

'A great deal, a great deal. All the countries where his church is dominant have excellent relations with the Palestinians and have gone out of their way to limit their contacts with Israel. Greece for example.'

I am stopped because I cannot argue with the partriarch's point; he's telling the truth. However, I find his refusal to answer questions about the abundance of monasteries and shortage of schools and his church's lack of involvement in everyday problems unacceptable. And his inability to speak Arabic is seen as an insult to the Greek Orthodox community which is deemed unable to produce its own local leadership.

I give up on him and decide to visit Father Thedoseus of the Greek Orthodox monastery of Bethany, someone I have known most of my life, to get a truer picture of things. After half an hour of pleasantries the hard questioning begins.

'Father Thedoseus, why doesn't your church do more to help the local Greek Orthodox community financially? They'll need help to survive.'

'We're a poor church, we have no money like the English church and the others.'

'Then politically, surely your church can use its offices overseas to publicize the plight of your people here.'

'We do . . .'

'I mean worldwide, not only in Greece.'

'We do. I mean, of course we do, after all Jewish soldiers beat me up personally, I told you about that last year [in 1969 two Israeli soldiers did in fact beat up the good father when he tried to stop them from entering his church]. They're very bad people, I mean the way they beat up children and the like. Of course, we do work against them.'

'What is the overall position of your church regarding the Palestinian question?'

'Believe me, we support the Palestinians, we've always supported the Palestinians, but there's very little we can do.'

Again, while the overall statement regarding Greek Orthodox support for the Palestinians may be true, the central point of whether it is making an issue of the suffering of its Holy Land community remains elusive. I cannot get an answer. The suspicion remains that a similar situation perpetrated by another state besides Israel would cause a greater outcry and a more intensive effort to discredit that state. There is no evidence that Greek Orthodox support for the Palestinian cause goes beyond the ordinary diplomatic effort, and there is considerable disturbing evidence that individual, even community-wide, cases of suffering do not receive the attention they deserve.

But the absence of a united Christian front goes further than the issue of a local church and its ability to influence a mother church; the local Christians manifest a distinct lack of faith in their local churches and their leadership. This is the direct result of Palestinian Christians refusing to accept their local churches' subscription to, or seeming acceptance of, the attitudes of Rome, Canterbury and Constantinople.

To social worker Rifaat Audeh, the local church has never represented anything except a 'Trojan Horse'. He accuses the church of representing an outside point of view 'which reflects the outside interests of where the church is located, the churches represent the West and not the local people. I find it appalling that some of the heads of the churches don't even speak Arabic.'

Jiryes Said Khoury, though careful to avoid direct criticism of any of the established churches, admits that 'the churches' presence in Jerusalem is symbolic, it has nothing to do with the local community'. And David Newhouse accuses the church of 'having resources that it doesn't use to help the people because it is more keen on continuing than on helping'.

I do verify that the lifestyle of the heads of the various churches points to a measure of insensitivity to the conditions of misery of their followers. And so do some of their actions and policies, including their acceptance of duty-free cars, courtesy of the State of Israel. The Greek Orthodox church's refusal to use some of its extensive land holdings to build housing for its own poor while using the same land holdings to maintain 'a presence' is but one shameful example of what is happening.

I reach the conclusion that, exceptionally, the Christian Embassy and the Zionist Christians are an open expression of a much larger Christian attitude of neglect towards Palestinian Christians. Most Christian churches behave as if they don't matter. Some of the believers in the Second Coming don't even know that Palestinian Christians exist, and others think a Christianity which doesn't believe in the Second Coming isn't worth saving, but most simply don't care.

Jimmy Swaggart, Jerry Falwell, Jim Bakker, Oral Roberts, Pat Newton and others believe 'Western Christian theology approves of the Zionist state'. To them and their followers Israel's 1967 victory was a miracle and the promised land is yet to be realized. Their statements are not far removed from what the others practice.

An unexpected opportunity to meet a great number of Christians and hear them talk about their problems, including the divisions among them, presented itself on 12 September 1991. Eighty-four Christians gathered at St George's Anglican Cathedral to attend a day-long seminar on 'War and the Theology of Liberation'. Two days before, the Protestant lawyer Jonathan Khuttab had told me, 'You'll learn a lot, all the people who're knowledgable and concerned will be there and they will discuss everything under the sun.' Jonathan was right.

The guests wandering around the beautifully manicured garden of St George's Cathedral are lawyers, professors, doctors, architects, priests, nuns, social workers and a high proportion of housewives. They represented a cross-section of the Christian community and the predominance of people in service businesses is a true reflection of their position in society. But even at 9.30 a.m. something beyond Christianity and middle-class white-collar status clings to them and it identifies them more than their religious affiliation and professional connections. They seem to suffer from an all-enveloping weariness which shows in the way they move, dress, talk and even hold copies of the programme of the seminar. In fact, a deep dispiritedness seems to be consuming them and it shows in each and every one of them. Their visible pain is their strongest bond.

We sit on the usual uncomfortable folding chairs in a large rectangular room and the seminar is opened by Canon Naim Ateeq, the energetic, grey-haired, gravelly-voiced preacher at St George's. He welcomes everybody to the seminar and yields to Anglican Archbishop Samir Kafity, appropriately the keynote speaker.

Kafity is a large man, well over six foot tall with broad shoulders, a thinning head of hair and an un-Arab red face; and he is wearing a large, seemingly heavy cross. Voice resounding throughout and finger pointing to heaven, Kafity doesn't mince his words. He marches into controversial territory in no time at all. 'Christ as a Jew is a fallacy perpetrated by the churches who have no sympathy with the Palestinians and want to deny the Palestinianism of Jesus.'

My on-the-spot notes, written in my usual irreverent style, contain the sentence. 'Kafity is going for the big prize; he wants to make Christ a Palestinian and deny his Jewish origins.' In fact, there is another more subtle aspect to the claim that Christ was a Palestinian, it represents a serious difference of opinion between the local church and its mother church in the West.

The rest of Kafity's brief speech identifies a problem I hadn't thought of. It is an appeal for restraint, a call to listeners to adhere to Christian teachings of non-violence, in the face of all the misery caused by the Israeli occupation. Canon Ateeq thanks the Archbishop and proceeds to deliver his own dissertation on the relationship of the individual to society and the state.

The audience looks fatigued, and I have the feeling that they have heard it all before and it doesn't work. Yet they're there, waiting for words to console them and, by the looks on their faces, having a hard time suppressing a cry for anything which would help them. Fifteen minutes later, Ateeq appears to deliver what is needed, a direct, unequivocal attack on the Western church. According to him, the Western church, indeed most Western Christians, do not sympathize with the Palestinian Christians. The attack is carried further and the Western church is accused of outright prejudice against the Christians of the East. Ateeq supports this contention by listing how the West changed Eastern Christian names to suit themselves (e.g. Boulus to Paul and Girges to George) and the distortion of historical fact such as the denial that

St George came from Lod in Palestine. (A few days later, in a separate interview, Ateeq confirms to me his belief that the problems of the Christians of Palestine are made in Rome, Constantinople and Canterbury.)

After lunch, and a satirical opening prayer which makes fun of the Israeli Prime Minister Itzhaq Shamir, the second speaker is Jonathan Khuttab, and he delivers an address on Christian Theology and the Idea of a Just War. This celebral sounding topic is considerably less so in a city where armed suppression is a way of life and where personal decisions can be easily validated (individual attack against Israelis by Christians are less frequent than ones by Muslims, but they take place). Even intellectually the topic is made more alive by such declarations as, 'The Christians are totally opposed to the idea of a chosen people.'

By the time the speakers finish and the question-and-answer session begins, two important things are already established. First, local Christian theology is markedly and seriously influenced by local conditions to the extent of producing a syncretic Christianity which espouses opinions which differ from those of the mother church. Second, the local Christians blame the churches in the West for many of their problems and for failing to help them against the Israelis and the conditions resulting from Israeli occupation.

Undoubtedly the question-and-answer session is more revealing than the carefully prepared speeches; for one thing the list of inter-Christian problems is much longer. Kafity, Ateeq and Khuttab limited themselves to pointing out some theological differences and to complaining about the Western churches' failure to help the local church. It is left to others to provide me with a dramatic reminder of the two other problems haunting local Christianity, identified by previous interviewees: the problems between the various churches and their consequent inability to bury the hatchet and get on together and the crisis of confidence between each local church and its followers. There are no satisfactory answers to the questions about the absence of a united Christian position and why the local churches aren't able to do more to influence their mother organizations; the answers amount to an appeal to the questioners to maintain a Christian attitude towards things.

In the process of revealing these two points the questioners expose several subsidiary but important points. The Christians of the Holy Land are great admirers of the radical South American church which is in the forefront of resisters to dictatorships and 'US economic colonialism' and would like to see their local churches adopt a similar policy. Most of the people attending the seminar are great admirers of Iraqi President Saddam Hussein because they credit him with creating a modern secular state which provides them with protection their churches haven't provided and stands in the way of the spread of the Islamic fundamentalist movement.

I leave the seminar totally committed to the idea that the most obvious fact of Christian life in the Holy Land is its separateness from the rest of Christianity. The feeling of helplessness it emits and its pervasive sadness are reflections of this.

The divisions in Christian ranks do take place at many levels and they complete the circle of non-acceptance which surrounds the Christian community of the Holy Land. Whether a unified Palestinian Christianity would be better prepared to face the problems of outside pressures is beyond doubt, what is less certain is whether it can do it alone without outside help. It is obvious that the local churches and the mother churches are far from blameless, but the local Christians are and they deserve sympathy, Christian and otherwise.

CHRISTIAN VOICES, CHRISTIAN FEARS

A GLIMMER OF HOPE

I am desperate for signs of hope, however small. As is often the case, hope resides with those who do not allow their pessimism to stand in the way of trying to correct things, to submerge their inherent belief. In this case, hope is more in what Camille Nassar does than in his unhappy prognosis. It is a situation where the critic–pessimist is trying to prove himself wrong.

'I want to talk to our people who run the Rehabilitation Centre; it's the only one of its kind in the territories, and with a little more help we could do much, much more. It'll give you an idea of the problems which exist and the type of practical steps needed to ease the guilt of misery, the agony and pain of our young people.'

Two days later I am in the company of Dena Asfour, the Hebrew-speaking public-relations officer and jack-of-all-trades for the YMCA Rehabilitation Centre. She drives me to the Group Centre at Beit Sahur, twelve miles south of Jerusalem. Dena briefs me on everything, talks impeccable English with the enthusiasm of the committed and confirms the obvious fact that she could be making more money and holding a job with a more promising future somewhere else. To minimize her sacrifice she tells me that most of the workers at the centre have served time in Israeli prisons and detention camps. She speaks of 'the joy of serving'. That and the fact that the Beit Sahur Group Centre houses forty-five to fifty girls and boys who've become handicapped as a result of *intifada*-related injuries is a happy story in itself, but it is only the tip of a bigger, happier picture.

Rifaat Audeh, the Group Centre's director, is a picture of the angry young ideologue who channels most of his anger into his work. Tall with a craggy, expressive face, he gives us coffee in his small office while launching a devastating attack on the Israelis, the Christian churches and the PLO in that order. 'Israel is a stupid theocracy which will eventually destroy itself. The only thing the Israeli state has going for it is its ability to adminster violence, and the West looks the other way because it's organized violence and they like things to be organized, they see state-administered violence differently from individual acts of violence.' This uncompromising summation of what Israel is and does is followed by an equally strong attack on the Christian churches. 'There are more churches there than there are Christians, practically a new church every day. Whenever they try to help, which is rare, they try to give our poor food. We don't want food, we want work. This is the voice of a simple Christian, but the churches are a failure, they should be a centre of resistance like the mosque, or they should emulate the South American church.' The suspicion that Audeh is a PLO operative promoting an ultra nationalist line is cancelled by his equally uncompromising dismissal of the PLO and its ways. 'They're nothing but a self-appointed, privileged group driving around European capitals in limousines. The cost of hiring a limousine for one day would make a substantial difference, a positive one, in the way this centre is run.'

I steer the conversation towards the activities of the centre, and Rifaat tells me that their programme fall into two distinct parts, vocational training and psychological counselling. We agree that the best way to understand these activities is to see them in practice and Rifaat takes me on a tour.

As we step out of the two-storey stone building in the middle of pine trees, I ask Rifaat where we are exactly and he tells me that we're a stone's throw from Shepherds' Field. I discover that the compound of the main two-story building surrounded by eight small houses occupies fourteen donums (about five acres) and that more houses are added whenever money becomes available. 'We handle as many people as we can, but it is a very small number of all who need both vocational training and psychological counselling. There are thousands of people out there who need help, somewhere between fourteen and seventeen thousand, but we simply don't have the facilities. Please keep in mind that while the organization is Christian, we do not discriminate in terms of our employees or guests, they come from all religions.'

The children receiving vocational training are attractive teenagers and some of them have missing limbs. Some are working on headboards for beds while others are tinkering with plumbing fixtures, training to maintain buildings and some of the girls are learning how to sew. In another building are other teenagers learning how to use IBM computers and yet others training to become secretaries and bookkeepers.

In total seven vocational training courses are available and moves are under way to add agriculture as a new discipline. Because of the demand on the centre's facilities, people are trained for only a period of three months. But even with that modest amount of training they're better equipped to find jobs than the rest of the people, certainly the rest of their age group. While no exact figures are available, Rifaat estimates that unemployment among their graduates is a quarter the national average.

During the tour to check on the vocational training activities, Dena Asfour tells me of the efforts to sell 'what the youngsters make' and how simple dolls, dresses and small coffee tables were attractively priced and found a ready market. The success of the children in making these items was such that an unnamed Israeli merchant had bought their products for a while but had to stop for political reasons. Dena makes her last comment as we're about to re-enter Rifaat's office and it prompts him to want to make a statement about how the Israelis view the centre and behave towards it. I prevail on him to wait until after we cover the psychological counselling programme, in some ways more of a pioneering effort than vocational training.

'It took a great deal to get parents to accept the fact that their children need psychological counselling. We have strong family ties in this part of the world and traditionally the family is responsible for the welfare of the children. But we were following a trial-and-error approach and we devised an approach to convince the parents that there is no shame in accepting what we do, particularly in view of the cause of the psychological problems, because they were the result of *intifada* activity.

'Our purpose is to help the children re-adjust to their physical and psychological wounds enough to have them reintegrated into the family and society as a whole. Very often this involves affording them vocational training to meet their new limitations.

'We can't afford individual counselling even when it is needed, we simply can't afford it. The length of time we keep someone here varies, essentially until we think they can be reintegrated. After that we send them home, but there is follow up by the Outreach programme.'

'What is the Outreach programme, Rifaat? – this is the first I've heard about it.'

'The Outreach programme follows up on what we do here, it checks on our graduates and works with them and their families. Sometimes the smallest bit of advice to the family on how to handle things makes a great deal of difference. The Outreach programme covers the whole West Bank through eight town centres and of course we're expanding it as the number of our graduates and the need increases. It's relatively new, started at the beginning of 1990, but it has been very successful so far.'

'Now that you have given me the full picture of the centre's work; do tell me how the Israelis view it.'

Dena, who knows all about this, leaves us together to do something else and Rifaat starts his tale of horror.

'The Israelis think of this as a centre for recycling terrorists. This isn't my description of the place, this is a phrase I heard some of them use to describe us. They don't like us, and they don't like what we do.

'They raided the place over a year ago. They marched in out of the blue without any provocation; I mean you've seen most of the place, is there anything in it to provoke? It was an evil act, more evil than most of what they do because most of the children we have are afraid of uniforms owing to what was done to them, what they suffered at the hands of Israeli soldiers. The ones, Israeli soldiers, who came into the centre beat up some of the staff, people who tried to stop them from wandering around and frightened the children, yes they actually beat them up. Then they confiscated the files to check on our activities, they took away the filing cabinets which contained nothing but the personal records of the children and indications of what progress they were making.

'What an experience, what a hideous experience. They haven't been in to give us a bad time for a while, but they harass some of our workers, they're always stopping them on their way home and giving them the third degree. And they drive back and forth in front of the place so the kids can see them and get upset.

'This place may be a danger to them, but not in the way they think. We are not recycling terrorists, but our vocational training programme is a long-term danger to them because we prove that given the smallest chance our young people can do well. They'll probably come to visit me after you print this, but go ahead and do it, I am accustomed to their ways.

'You know how ridiculous they can get, do you? Well one of the times they came here they issued a directive that the children here are not to paint slogans or flags, and they aren't to sing nationalistic songs. The simple fact is that no one has ever done any of these things. We aren't in that business anyway, but it gives you an idea of how silly they are and how worried they are.'

'It does sound hideous. But, I want to follow up on something else, Rifaat, I want to know more of what happens to people after they receive their vocational training?'

'They get jobs, I think I told you. If you're talking about their political commitment, then that's up to them and we have nothing to do with it. I promise you that we're not into that, it would be totally self-defeating to get into anything except what we do. In this part of the world doing something constructive is the ultimate revolution and I am into that to my ears. I certainly think I am doing something constructive, instead of something political and stupid.'

'I accept that, but where do they go, how well do they do, what happens to them?'

'Come back in a few years, it's much too early for that because we only started two years ago. But, if they leave us alone then we'll have an impact, maybe small or maybe big, but an impact. Vocational training is what we need, much more than universities. We have enough universities and college graduates, we need people with vocational training, that's what will change the infrastructure.'

We break for lunch and eat cafeteria-style in the small functional dining area in the main building. The food is wholesome, the same which is served to the residents. As we're continuing our discussion one of the assistants tells Rifaat that the guests are there. Rifaat asks the assistant to bring them and asks to me stay for the meeting.

The guests turn out to be an eight-person group, the 1991 Veterans' Delegation to the Middle East. The former members of the US armed forces are committed to 'the non-violent pursuit of justice' and their fact-finding mission has as its purpose learning more about the public organizations whose aim is the furtherance of peace.

Most members of the group are dressed in army-type khaki uniforms. They very politely query Dena and Rifaat about the function, history and hopes of the centre and get answers similar to ones I had heard myself. They profess open admiration for what the centre is doing and ask specific questions about how they might help. Eventually they ask if they can go on a tour of the centre and I decide to join them. A messenger is sent ahead to explain who the visitors are to guard against any adverse reaction to their military uniforms.

We go to one room where boys and girls are painting and where they have some of their previous work on the walls. Instead of the slogans and flags the Israelis worry about, most of their paintings have a dove or the word peace or both in them. In a corner, there are reproductions of churches and mosques and there are some dolls and headbands. I notice a bulletin board full of notices of events and pictures of previous visitors and postcards from them. And also on it, next to the testaments of friendship and love, are the identity cards of all the residents – just in case Israeli army patrols come in and ask what the place and the other people in it are all about.

After we finish with the art room we go into a cottage where a worker, a counsellor, is reading English to a one-legged boy. She tells us that she's helping him with his studies and refuses to identify herself beyond telling us she's a Dutch volunteer and her name is Youlanda. By the time we finish our tour it is late afternoon and somehow the Centre's proximity to Shepherds' Field is felt by all of us, a strange sense of peace descends on the place. Dena and I bid everybody farewell and drive back to Jerusalem.

'Dena, where does the money for the centre, for the whole programme, come from?'

'From the European Church Group, Christian Aid in the UK, Medical Aid to the Palestinians also in the UK and the Danish Church. But there are others who give once in a while.'

'By the looks of things, it would take little money to help.'

'Yes, I am not involved in that, but most definitely yes.'

'Well, Dena, I now know why you have forgone better opportunities elsewhere.'

She smiles knowingly. 'I am attached to Palestine, most of all to Jerusalem and I am certainly attached to this.' The 'this' in her hand was a little doll one of the girls at the centre had given her.

The two times I go to see Doris Salah she looks harried and very tired, but that doesn't stop her from giving me all the time I need. Her looks, commitment to hard work and generosity of spirit all remind me of my late mother and though I never disclose this to Doris we do get along very well and I believe that she is much more forthcoming talking to me than with 'any old interviewer'.

Doris is the director of the YWCA, the sister organization of the YMCA but totally independent. The fact that she and her organization are my second examples of what can be done is an accident, totally unrelated to my contact with the YMCA, and, if anything, both examples go a long way towards proving that constructive work is quite possible, if only people would try.

We're in one of the lecture halls of the YWCA, a large stone building off the main thoroughfare of the Arab part of Jerusalem, and we're alone. There are tables, benches and chairs everywhere; it is a place where a lot of activity normally takes place. Doris Salah is answering my first question.

'We're involved in relief work, educational work, vocational training and subsidiary extensions of these activities like the placement of people in jobs and the sale of products made by vocational trainees.'

Doris continues and tells me that very much like its sister organization the YWCA doesn't admit people on the basis of religious affiliation. She smiles, saying, 'A lot of the time I have no idea to what religion some of the students belong, and I actually don't care, I am much more interested in how well or badly they're doing and if there is more we can do for them.'

The education programme conducted by the YWCA operates on many levels and in many places. Their teachers work with 250 four- to six-year-olds in refugee camps such as Akbat Jabr, Jalazoun and Kalandia and they very often work with the mothers to teach them embroidery, knitting and other crafts. 'We got some of the refugees into small-scale food production and of course we sell the food – marmalade and some local specialities – for them. I don't know if this is going to grow into something big, but I am not sure that's what matters, what matters is that it's happening.

'Here [in the Sheikh Jarrah headquarters in Jerusalem], we manage the most ambitious secretarial training programme in the whole of the occupied territories. People join this programme from all over the territories, the number of trainees fluctuates between 150 and 200, and many of them obtain scholarships and go overseas to continue their studies. We try to help them obtain scholarships, mostly in European countries; the US doesn't do much in this area.'

'But you have other programmes beside the secretarial programme, don't you?'

'Oh yes, many. The secretarial programme is the big one, it straddles the vocational and educational. But we have classes for dress-making, home-making, nutrition, and other straightforward subjects like languages, etc.'

'You must have a huge staff, how many people do you have?'

Doris laughs, puffs on her cigarette and looks straight at me. 'We have to make do with what we have; we have thirty-two people in the field and a few more here, but of course those here included a lot of administrative people and others who aren't involved in outside activities.

'By the way, I forgot to tell you that the courses people take here involve the payment of a tuition fee, but it is subsidized. Also it is very competitive – everybody wants to join our courses and there simply isn't enough room.'

'You've talked about educational and vocational training but very little about relief work. What does that entail?'

'Relief work is to help people cope, particularly refugees. We're talking about families where the mother can't cope because she's having another child and about cases of direct relief due to poverty. We don't like the basic idea of charity work, but if it is needed then it is needed; I mean we'd rather be helpful in a more permanent problem-solving way.'

'Now, tell me why the churches aren't doing something similar to what you're doing?'

'I don't think that's correct, there are churches which are extremely helpful in their own ways. The Quakers help pay the costs of defending youngsters in courts of law, the Mennonites and others help, and of course there are the various medical aid programmes from Britain, Sweden, Italy and other countries.'

'Interestingly you haven't mentioned one of the local churches?'

She smiles knowingly. 'But I thought you knew all about them. They're mostly in education, but they do an excellent job there. Where would we be without St George's School and Freres College – and indeed Bethelehem University was started by the Roman Catholic church.'

'Let me backtrack. We have a special situation which needs a particular response, I mean you definitely need more vocational training and fewer college graduates, and the churches aren't doing anything about that.'

'They do educate, perhaps the other areas are not for them.'

'I am going to stay on this area. The churches still spend a lot of money managing their properties and there are more priests and monasteries than one can count, but there are no church-run vocational centres, nor is the church interested in things of this type. Why?'

The happy smile of the blameless covers her face, cigarette smoke is everywhere and she recrosses her legs. 'I don't think it's for me to comment on anything except on what we do. This place and what it does for other people are my concern.'

'Now, let me know about the people with whom you work, the girls to be exact.'

'No, the type of people in the refugee camps and who need relief is undoubtedly known to you. I think you're talking about the people with whom we work here, at headquarters. The girls are mostly in their late teens, average representatives of our middle class, they come from families who would allow girls to work and they themselves are very desirous to lead their own lives and to contribute.'

'What do they feel about life? It must be difficult to come to classes past the Israeli patrol standing at the corner. How do they feel about things like that?'

'Well most of the girls we have were born after the Israeli occupation of '67. They have never known freedom; they were born under Israeli occupation and continue to live under it. Thank God, they're able to take stress; we see no overt signs of trauma, perhaps it's easier for people born in these conditions than others.'

We both laugh. 'Doris, I can't help it, I have to return to comparisons. Whatever message the church, or the local churches, transmit about conditions in the occupied territories doesn't get there, to the outside world. I am not sure it's their fault, it could be the fault of those who receive the message, the mother churches. In either case, your own message, what you're doing here is a different kind of message, but it is one that can't be hidden, it's there. Is the message about what you're doing reaching the outside world?'

'I think so, I certainly hope so. We are part of the Y worldwide, and we have delegations coming here from all over the world in a little over a month. They'll be able to see for themselves and they'll tell the world what we do and what is going on here.'

'These are people from the Y worldwide?'

'Yes.'

'And are they the people who support you?'

'Yes, directly and indirectly and in every way. They provide us with funds to do what we do and they were among the first to speak out on the question of human rights in the occupied territories. We send them status reports which they circulate to branches of the Y worldwide who try to do as much as possible to spread the message.'

My next question is answered, off the record, and so is the one which follows and we decide to continue our conversation on this basis. It isn't that Doris Salah is highly political or inflammatory, far from it; she is a totally constructive person with nothing to hide. It is just a simple wish on my part to protect the place and those who work in it from the fears of those who see sinister designs even in the simplest acts of the kindest people.

The examples of the Rehabilitation Centre and the YWCA are clear evidence that much is possible and attainable and that self-help channels exist on the ground. Both organizations have been operating in the Holy Land since the turn of the century, originally as recreation centres and to provide inexpensive lodging for travellers. They have no specific church affiliation, live off donations received from many sources and are committed to doing rather than to preaching. Both changed with the times and keep evolving to meet the needs of the people. And though the word Christian is part of their names, they directed their efforts towards the whole community and through that improved the lot of the Palestinian Christians and contributed to greater Muslim–Christian understanding. While Doris Salah is too polite to enter into a comparative discussion, her own obvious success underscores the failure of others.

THE TRIUMPH OF CHRISTIAN OPTIMISM

The contributions of Doris Salah and Camille Nassar show me that there is room for constructive action of the type which eludes most churches and groups. It doesn't take me long to find an independent Christian contributor to the welfare of his people, someone who doesn't have the benefit of an outside organization with a global reach.

He is consumed by a healthy anger, driven by an inner conviction which challenges everything and everybody around him. And he wears his successes with an enchanting natural elegance, free of the locals' penchant for self-praise, and goes forward to do more. Above all, Jad Izhaq doesn't care whether he is a Christian Palestinian or Palestinian Christian, whatever ground he occupies is acceptable to him so long as it permits him to 'serve'. I had met him before, on a previous trip, and came out envious, wishing I could do more than write. I am on my way to see him again, with the nervousness which accompanies meeting those whose very existence is a reproach to our shortcomings. I liken him to a saint, then, thinking of what he does, to a girl who looks good no matter what she wears and what she does. The comparisons don't work because he is a product of his environment, an extension of the best in the land where he lives. He is a Christian and a gentleman, and I use both descriptive words spaciously, without qualifications.

There is a dusty stretch of road from the taxi stop on the Jerusalem to Bethlehem thoroughfare to his modest three-room office and it is early afternoon and unbearably hot. It is located on the ground floor of a small house, but the strong commitment to doing things without generating noise is apparent and there are no signs to identify it and hardly a sign of life.

We greet each other warmly. I am introduced to the young man visiting him, surmise that their business is unfinished and volunteer to wait. Jad is telling his young colleague how to pursue a research project. 'We have to determine that they can do the work. I don't want the project to fail, so we must determine whether they have the right people to do what is required. Otherwise, it's all a waste of time.'

The project in question is one for making clothes, a small operation which would employ ten people, but he is making sure that the ladies to be hired from the local village can sew to specifications. His instructions to the attentive researcher reveal other practical aspects which tell me much about his approach: getting women from other places would defeat the purpose of helping the community where the project is located and there are no facilities to train people. The Applied Research Institute which Jad Izhaq directs – one of the many hats he wears – is in the business of researching and implementing cottage industries like this one.

I think of my last trip to see him; how he had arrived uncharacteristically late. He had been at Bethlehem University, where he is chairman of the Department of Life Sciences, talking to students who wanted to riot in protest over the arrest of some of their mates. 'I had to convince them that their action would constitute an excuse for the Israeli authorities to shut down the university, once again. It took a bit of work, but they accepted my point of view that rioting would be counterproductive. They're good lads; they listen to reason.' I listened to him tell the story and noted that there was no hint of tiredness or exasperation and no exaggeration of the problem he faced or of his role, only a matter-of-fact recitation of what the situation was all about by way of apology for his lateness.

This time he finishes briefing his colleague and turns to me with eager friendly eyes. 'Are you in a real hurry? If you aren't then let's take a ride. There is something I want you to see.' The invitation is accepted and we drive through Bethlehem and are on our way to Beit Sahur, his home town. We're talking about my last book *Cry Palestine*, and the reception it got. Suddenly he takes a sharp turn and points to what looks like a small shop.

'I can't stop because we don't have the time. That's the old Jordan Plastic Company [named when Jordan controlled the West Bank]. It makes a number of plastic products: chairs, tables, kitchen stuff, quite a number of things. It's owned by the Abu Aitah family; they're locals. It's a living example of the kind of small industry we need. Why import this kind of thing when it can be made here at a much lower price. There is no end to the kind of small businesses like this that we can use, where the talent to make the product and the market are available. Look at it this way: it makes sense to an investor, it creates employment and it produces much needed products at lower prices.'

I take notes as he speaks and gestures while driving and soon we're in the middle of Beit Sahur, the town which was placed under day-and-night curfew for fifty-four days because its citizens refused to pay Israeli taxes. He parks his car in an alley and marches into a small house built early in the century and I follow behind him.

I look at the gadgets around in the first room we enter, the small wooden cradle, the huge cast-iron pot, an ancient sewing machine and turn-of-the-century pictures and pamphlets on the walls. In the second room are more memorabilia and small wicker baskets and boxes and artifacts made of olive wood. I am transported to Bethlehem and Beit Sahur some time before the First World War, and he confirms my assessment and tells me that the place, except for the items for sale, is a recreation of a typical home, a folkloric museum of sorts.

'We call it *aseel*; it's a typical, ideal Beit Sahur home of earlier this century, real, without any glamorization. We want people to recall their roots and be proud, to think of the simple close-to-the-earth life the ancestors lived. Look at this picture. The man on the right is my grandfather, and the rest of the people are members of the village council. A lot of people are surprised that we had a village council, but we did; it functioned quite well enough and divided the land into eight equal shares for people to live off; it represented the people and was beholden to them. Look at this brass coffee grinder, I think it still works. It was fun seeing this place come into being. Look at that *kanoon* [brazier], it was the only thing which kept them warm. What do you think?'

I am impressed by the charm of the place and the thinking behind it. Many of the items exhibited are similar to ones I grew up with in Bethany, and I agree that they conjure up a solid way of life which is no more. 'So this place is to make people aware of their heritage, to give them something to hold on to?'

'Yes, that was the original purpose and it worked very well – people loved it, it's a piece of constructive nostalgia. Then we decided to open up to outsiders, to tourists and visitors, to show them what we were all about. And it is a success with outsiders as well, we have many tourist groups which come here and it wets their appetites; by the time they're finished here they want to learn more about us. It counters the image of us as uncivilized savages.'

'How do you fund it, Jad?'

'We have two girls who run the whole show, that one there is one of them. We make a little money selling the little things you saw and that's all we need. So far so good, but if tourism ever dies on us then I'll still keep it going, even if I have to sell my house. I am so proud of it.'

In fact his house is only around the corner and we go there for a cup of coffee. His sons and daughter (Firas, Fady, Usama and Dima) have just come home from school and the man's love affair with life and doing what matters shows in his affectionate fatherly manner and the way he asks them about whether they've done their homework and the attractive exchange which follows.

It is a comfortable house without trimmings, perhaps with a little more glassware and more books than in similar homes.

He apologizes for his wife Ghada's absence and asks me how my research is coming along.

'Well, quite well, but the problems of the Christians of the Holy Land are greater and much more complex than I had anticipated. I am here to listen to you. How does the Christian minority's problem look to you?'

'I think we should agree on the terms we use before I can help you. I am not a minority, to me a minority is a small group which doesn't belong, and I assure you that I don't feel that way. You could call me an Islamic Christian and get away with it because the basic way of life in this part of the world is Muslim. But we've been here for ages, continuously since 1635, and we've never been involved in conflicts, divisions or any of that nonsense, nothing that would make us feel like a minority. Beit Sahur is a mixed community of Christians and Muslims and I challenge anybody to point out any problems we have ever had. Even the Christian settlers, the ones who came here with the Crusades, have been Arabized and you can't distinguish them enough to call them outsiders or a minority. Look at Hanna Seniora [a Roman Catholic nationalist leader], they don't come more Arab than him. Don't get Hanna upset by calling him a minority.'

Our laughter has a happy ring to it. I totally accept his basic notion and applaud the concept that the label minority is a crippling one which implies problems. 'Your attitude and all the things you do represent a blast of fresh air. What I get from other people is a feeling of helplessness and the closer to the church one gets the stronger it is. What's behind that?'

'You've put your finger on one of our major problems. The church is torn between its responsibility to the people and its allegiance to the mother churches. With minor exceptions the mother churches are all Western, and the people who run them, even when they're Arabs, are into maintaining a balancing act which saps their energies and vitiates their effectiveness. There's nothing wrong with the Western churches if you're leading a happy normal life, if you have independence; but their teachings, which reflect the conditions under which people live, have very little to do with the special situation of the Christians here, how *we* live

and what *we* suffer. Extend this; think of the church as a
traditional establishment and think of our conditions as
requiring inventiveness and forward-thinking and the
problem becomes clear. I am sure you've heard it before; this
is why people here are looking for a model to follow and
their model is the revolutionary church in South America,
the church which became a vehicle for change to meet the
particular circumstances hounding it.'

'So the way of the church doesn't work?'

'The way, strategy, of the church is wrong – judged by the
people. I mean this is not the time for sectarian church
schools, this is a time which doesn't afford us the luxury of
emphasizing a Catholic or Protestant point of view, and
schools should be for everybody. And it goes further, much
deeper. By responding to the mother churches the local
churches have made the local Christians schizoid, divided
between wanting to stay with their church and their loyalties
to the needs of their compatriots, the average people.'

'The way you talk I am tempted to think the problem
within the Christian community and what the churches stand
for comes ahead of the other problems, the ones with Israel
and Islamic fundamentalism. Is that true?'

'No, not in the case of Israel. Israel is manifestly anti-
Christian and whether this is policy or not matters little
because that's the way it comes through, that is the hard
reality. If Israel needs anything from us then it is ignorant
workers, labourers, and most of the Christians don't qualify
because they're educated so why the devil should they want
them? They want what serves their purposes, servants and
builders, and the Christians don't fit their requirement.
Think of it, they have no use for thinking Christians who
know their rights and what they're entitled to and ask for this
in an open, educated way which they can't suppress because
it doesn't involve violence or similar things which would
allow them to react against them in their usual harsh way.
The Christian-led revolt against paying taxes is a greater
threat to the Israelis than someone wielding a knife.

'Now to the Muslim problem, which some people are fond
of pointing out. To me, it doesn't exist, I don't see it. There is

a problem, a social problem, because the churches are going West while the Muslims are going East, but the remedy is not to complain about the Muslim fundamentalists, the remedy is for the Christians to go East where they belong.

'I have no idea why my church is called the Greek Orthodox Church and not the Eastern Orthodox Church. I don't dislike Greece, the Greeks are our friends, but what's Greece go to do with me? Why am I neglected in this mix of religion and nationality? I have no idea; certainly there is no justification for saying *kiree ye lyseen* instead of *ya rab allah*. If I complain about that as a son of the church then others are entitled to make the same complaint.'

'Suppose we leave the churches alone. What would happen if the Christians stayed with the tourist business but stopped relying on their relationship with the church for help? What would attaining economic independence that way do?'

'It would perpetuate the social problem of the Christian in a different way and for different reasons. If the division with the Muslims now, whatever of it exists, is because of the Western pull of the church, then having a prosperous Christian community would create another type of division because the others, Muslims, have little to do with tourism and don't have any money. It would become a class struggle between haves and have-nots and the haves would really be threatened.'

'Are you telling me that the two major avenues, church help and tourism, leading to a better life for the Christian would also lead to alienation from their Muslim compatriots?'

'If these avenues are greater church help directed exclusively at the Christians or at improving an exclusively Christian business like tourism, then the answer is an unqualified yes. Whatever is done for and by the Christians must affect the community as a whole or they will suffer for it.'

'Like what? What would help the community as a whole?'

'Goodness, there are so many things, but I will start with things that should be done to the local church to make it a more effective instrument for and by the people. Changing the churches this way would place them where they belong, as the source of guidance and comfort to the people.

'The first thing any local church should do is to become Arabized and liberated. But that means it should belong to the people here, be an extension of them, responsive to their concerns. In deciding to respond to people's concerns the church will find out what to do, it will discover that it has to protect the Christian presence here. To me, and I emphasize that this is a personal opinion, this involves a number of things. The church must give the people pride in their Arab origins through a back-to-the-land movement. As the biggest landowner and a source of financial help, the church must support the creation of small businesses. The church must deal with our relations with our brother Muslims realistically. We must be close to them as in the past and not alien to them. The church must see fit to support a move back to the extended family and tribalism. It sounds archaic, but it has served us well in the past.'

'Right, let's go through some of these things and how they might be pursued.'

'Said, not today, my friend. I have some people coming to see me at the office. We'll have to meet again. I'll call you as soon as I know what I am doing next week.'

Two days later Jad telephones and leaves me a message at my hotel. The man who hands me his message is one of his former students, and he goes out of his way to tell me what a great man his former professor is. 'Mr Aburish, if you're seeing him again, please convey my respects.'

I deliver the message the following day, while Jad and I are continuing our discussion in his office.

'Right, can we go through the points you made as to what the church should do?'

Jad laughs at my exact recollection of where we left off. 'May I do it my way, Said? I want to do it in a way which would make sense to everybody, even the simplest reader.

'Close your eyes and think of Cyprus, the Greek part of it, not the fact that it's divided and has ethnic problems, but as a success story. What have we got there? We've got a people who're very close to the land, to what they have. It's so much in the air you can almost feel it. You have people who're great believers in the family as a constructive unit, and naturally beyond that the bigger unit, town or tribe. There the church isn't pulling in a different direction. This leads to a substantial reduction in the social tensions. Small businesses are flourishing in Cyprus, anything from making wine to vegetable packing and even subsidiaries of the tourist business. Cyprus is also one of the financial centres for the Middle East. In other words, Cyprus is a success story. And you know why? Above all, because they aren't saddled with our problems.

'My friend, Cyprus did all this without having a single university. What Cyprus has is democracy, not a tyrannical state which makes it its business to stifle initiative, and it has enterprise and a situation where the church and the people are heading in the same direction. There's a way to do it, there's a way to emulate Cyprus despite all the hurdles – and, damn the Israelis, they're good at placing them in the way of the people. They're so determined to control the tourist business they stopped Bethlehem University from starting several programmes to educate people in providing better services. We have so much talent here, we have a lot of wasted talent, and with that we can make the loaf of bread and don't have to beg for it. Who the hell wants charity? Old-fashioned charity is all the church can think of.'

'Jad, I've been listening to you and to other people and there is one thing I can't understand: why not go it alone without the church? Why do you need the church?'

'I hope you don't think that I am enamoured of any church, but there are solid reasons why they're needed, unfortunately. We, the Palestinians, need a body here to represent us. Of course, the PLO does; I am talking about representing us in terms of day-to-day issues, things the Israelis don't permit the PLO to do. The church has always been our point of contact with the outside world, and the absence of another body to do the job has strengthened them in this role. Even without the PLO connection, we could create the bodies to do the job but the Israelis would suppress them. So we're stuck with an old ineffective vehicle, the church.

'Don't forget that the church have considerable local power because they are the largest landowners we have. You see under Turkey the Christians couldn't own land so they registered whatever land they bought in the name of the church and some people got carried away and started giving the church land as presents. So . . . they own a hell of a lot of land. And they control education and so on. There is no end to their misery.'

Jad's thinking about the church and what needs to be done, Muslim–Christian relations and dealing with the other ills afflicting the occupied territories is so clear, I decide to retreat into talk about his work.

'What do your various study and other groups do?'

He laughs, and though it's at my expense, it's infectious.

'What don't we do? We do everything. Let me rephrase that; we try to do everything, but whether we succeed or not is something for other people to judge.

'We're in the business of creating self-confidence and self-reliance. This is the function of a much-needed planning commission, but we don't have one. We work with what is available. Beyond the human factor what we have is agriculture, small industries, tourism and other services businesses. Of course we try to train people in areas which are vital to our continuance, in the areas of health care, civil administration, municipal planning and the like.

'In agriculture we try to teach people to rotate crops and introduce new ones. We teach people better ways to take care of livestock, and of course we're involved in the various stages of marketing what people produce and decisions such as whether they should sell the product fresh or canned. There are lots of committed young people involved in these efforts and they do a good job. Now people grow guava instead of too much okra, cheeses are made more efficiently and hygienically, and coffee is canned. The Bedouins get more out of their livestock now, and it didn't take a great deal to educate them in how to take care of their flocks.

'In small industries, there is great potential in the clothing area. We already have over thirty thousand people working in this business, but there is no reason why this can't be much

bigger. We even have people who write software programmes for computers and the programmes are used in
Arab countries. There is potential in handicrafts. The soap
business is another area and a very good one.

'Then there is tourism, and you can't escape it. We have
more attractions in this area than . . . you name it. Let's
convert the sources of the dispute to a source of income – the
Church of the Holy Sepulchre, Dome of the Rock and
Wailing Wall. Is there any place like the old city of
Jerusalem, or any other Bethlehem? If we develop the
structure of this business then there is enough for everybody
and its success won't cause problems. Think of the follow up
in the hotel, tourist shop and restaurant areas. Why can't
people have a second home here the way they do in places
like Cyprus? The Dead Sea offers immense development
potential. This is a place where people can come to winter, or
to summer, or to see the sights and have fun, and it is
relatively cheap – by what I hear, very cheap.

'The service-businesses area is one people don't associate
with us, but it is one of tremendous potential. Believe me,
financial institutions could thrive here; after all, our people
are the bankers of the Middle East. Our people are also the
consultants in the Middle East, most of the engineering
consultancy, accounting firms and business consultancies in
the area are Palestinian. Even in education we could become
a centre, with our various universities, and we have a head
start in vocational centres. I'd like to see us become the
computer centre for the whole Middle East.

'The potential exists in all these areas, a few thousand
dollars can make all the difference in the world.'

'What you talk about is impressive, but it isn't exclusively
Christian. Where do the Christians fit in?'

'They fit in through contributing to the whole picture, not
by sitting in a corner and talking about being a minority. We
have a chance to lead and through that to serve the whole.
We have to provide the educators, thinkers and technicians,
to be the vanguard of change and this is where the church
comes in. The church should lead.'

'Are you saying constructive Christian action would

change the situation of the Christian and the rest of the people?'

'I am saying that constructive Christian action is the only way. Naturally, we would like the world to stop the Israelis from putting hurdles in our way.'

I remember that Jad's academic credentials include studies at Egyptian, American and British universities and this makes him qualified to answer my follow-up question. 'Is this your message to the outside world?'

'Yes, it is. We want them to give us a chance to prove ourselves by eliminating the pressures which keep us down and with every little help we can stand on our own feet. A combination of these two things would be to allow companies in Europe to invest here.'

'And what is your message to the outside church?'

'They should know the esssence of true Christianity. Their view of what should be done and how is distorted. They should re-learn the essence of Christianity from us, from our response in the face of adversity.'

'What about the local church?'

'I've said enough. But I'll repeat that they should concentrate on their own people, and I mean all their people. They should focus on pride in local Christianity and in their Palestinianism and the good things they have acquired from their Muslim culture.'

'Any messages to the PLO?'

'No. Abu Ammar [Yassar Arafat] knows the problem very well. It's sad he isn't allowed to do more about it.'

Our latest meeting ends with a discussion of the many papers he has written about agriculture, health and industry in the occupied territories and I note with utter enchantment that one of them dealt with Palestinian flora and what is required to save it. I leave Jad Izhaq as he's planning to meet with a Lutheran reprsentative about their vocational training centre, thinking of the next issue of the *Bethlehem University Journal* and talking to an engineer about his efforts to help the Rashaidah Bedouins with their sheep. I carry with me the feeling of envy which I developed when I met him before and a sincere wish that I haven't taken up too much of his valuable time.

THE POLITICIAN – HANAN ASHRAWI

To many of my friends who see the Middle East from a distance, she's 'the Palestinian woman who speaks so elegantly', 'the nice lady who's on TV all the time' or 'the wonderful Palestinian woman at the peace conference'. Western politicians and newsmen aren't far behind in their praise. To many Arabs she's 'Dr Hanan Ashrawi', a term of address which carries with it some reservations to do with her sex and her religion. But adoring Palestinians cast all doubts aside and call her 'Hanan' and they pronounce her name in an affectionate way giving it a rare depth of meaning; her name lends itself because it means 'affection'.

She's Hanan to me also, a new but already valued friend whom I have watched from a distance for some time. In fact, to me, it is the quality of her voice which tells her story, much more so than the recognized elegance of her words. It is a fractured voice which holds a strange balance between certainty and doubt, in her case it is the courage of her doubts which comes through to me. I find this apt, remarkably fitting, for even when they don't admit it the Palestinian Christians are caught between total commitment to Palestine and serious doubts about their future, as a community and religiously.

But I know Hanan Mikhael-Ashrawi – the full name and hyphenation are hers – well enough to know that she places her Palestinianism above all, so it is only appropriate that I assess her on her accepted identity, as the new and admired voice of the Palestinians. For a whole day in London, on 2 June 1992, I tried to observe her at close range by following her breakneck schedule. Her day began at 7:30 a.m. with an interview on *Today* for the BBC's Radio 4. Later that morning she gave interviews to Agence France Prsse, the BBC World Service Radio and TV, Reuters and Sky TV. In each case the questions were thought out and tough and she handled them with the finesse of an agile footballer entertaining the neighbourhood kids. She finished in time to rush to have dinner with Sir Ian Gilmour, the former diplomat and Middle East expert.

After lunch she spent the afternoon preparing a statement which she later delivered to a select group at the House of Commons. This was followed by questions, friendly and otherwise, which she handled with skill. During several subsequent interviews, which had the benefit of what had transpired, she had to field a question by the *Independent*'s Patrick Cockburn regarding her availability as a possible leadership alternative to the PLO's Yasser Arafat. She answered it with a captivating smile.

My notes from the early hours of the morning tell very little. She's the youngest of four girls; she's in her middle years; she's the wife of a photographer, who shuns the limelight, and the mother of two teenage girls, one of whom is on an exchange programme in London; and she's remarkably attractive. I don't know whether she's pretty, but pretty or not is subordinated to the human warmth she undoubtedly emits. Hanan Ashrawi is capable of giving a simple hug extra meaning – but she needs a prop, she smokes more than two packets of cigarettes a day.

Beyond these personal characteristics, she was (and officially still is), before she attained fame and earned her adjectives, the head of the Religious Affairs Department of Beir Zeit University, the largest institution of higher education in the occupied territories. Her educational qualifications include a bachelor's degree from the American University of Beirut and a PhD in medieval literature from the University of Virginia. But academic qualifications aside, what matters is how a forty-six-year old Episcopalian managed this position in a mostly Muslim university.

By all accounts, Hanan Ashrawi's classes weren't only well-attended, they were extremely popular with the students. Her approach appears to have been matter of fact and she brought her superior learning to bear on an otherwise tedious subject and transformed it into a 'fun course'. A former student speaks of her 'dealing with how these remote things affect our lives' and an admiring female colleague at Bethlehem University, Mae Nassar, recalled her to explain the new role for women, 'Hanan is the model for all of us.'

These admiring comments are shared by outsiders, and British Council head Chris McConville, a man who dealt with her as a member of a scholarship committee, views her present success without surprise. 'The moment she became part of the Palestinian Delegation to the Peace Conference, I kept my fingers crossed that they would give her a chance to show herself. They did, and look at the result, what a Palestinian woman with a cigarette holder can do.'

Indeed, the results are there for everybody to see. She is one of the most familiar faces on international television, and certainly one of the most admired. But, as usual, this has come at a considerable cost. Her London routine on 2 June was not the tolerable once-in-a-great-while happening, it is what her life has become, and to be under this type of constant pressure and to wear it well without once losing her cool, is extremely remarkable. In the past five months alone, she's been to London three times, Washington twice, Madrid, Athens, Rome, Cairo, Amman and several other cities and in each the performance repeats itself. Even when at home, the telephone never stops ringing. 'The most difficult parts are my absences from my family,' she told the Sky TV interviewer after she had overwhelmed him with her remarkable knowledge of what is involved in the peace process. The man nodded sympathetic understanding.

But reverence – and that is what I have for her performance as a spokesperson for the Palestinians – cannot be allowed to stand in the way of getting to the bottom of a story. And so I began my interview with Hanan by giving her an outline of the idea of this book.

'I don't like to answer questions about religion; for the Palestinians it is a side-issue, the overall Palestinian problem comes first,' was her reaction.

'But my intended book is about the Christians of the Holy Land and it has to make mention of their leading representative. Religion is what the book is all about, it's at the core.' I set the record straight while remembering that her assistant, Suheil Al-Baha, had not known what her religious affiliation was, a dramatic confirmation that Hanan does indeed place religion well behind nationality. 'If you prefer, let us begin with political questions and cover religion later. In view of the fact that the Islamic fundamentalist movement in the occupied territories and two major political movements, the Popular Front for the Liberation of Palestine and the Democratic Front for the Liberation of Palestine, are opposed to the present negotiations with the Israelis, the peace conference or process, then do you still feel that you have a mandate to negotiate with Israel?'

'The mandate of the Palestinian delegation to the peace process is clear: it derives from binding decisions taken by our highest representative and democratic bodies, the Palestine National Council, the PLO Executive Committee and the PLO Central Council. These bodies have reaffirmed the mandate when appropriate, the Central Council recently reaffirmed Palestinian participation during its May 1992 meeting by majority decision. Palestinian democracy, however, includes the right to oppose these decisions, and we will defend the opposition's right to present their point of view in accordance with the principle of free speech and mutual respect. Their [the opposition's] scepticism is understandable, given the constraints and unjust conditions placed on the Palestinians. Nevertheless, the imperatives of peace demand that we go foward with the grave responsibility of insuring Palestinian self-determination through the current negotiations.'

I pause to look at my notes only to discover that Hanan's standard answer for whether she will see peace in her lifetime is a simple, 'I hope so.' I find it difficult to ask for more. Still, the pregnant long answer merits analysis. The supremacy of the democratic process is evoked, without reservations. Simultaneously, it is obvious that Hanan Ashrawi feels the misgivings of others opposed to the peace process, of those who believe that you can't deal with Israel when it behaves in a fashion not conducive to producing positive results, particularly in the area of continuing to build new settlements. Hanan leaves the door open for the decision to participate in the peace process to be rescinded.

Having conceded that, the description of the Palestine National Council and the PLO Executive Committee as democratic bodies is, to me, highly questionable. Not only are the Muslim fundamentalists not represented on them – and they easily have the support of twenty-five per cent of the population – but most of the people who sit on these bodies are Arafat appointees who are not elected by the people. Still, there is no doubt that a majority of the Palestinian people wish to continue with the peace process and support the PLO decisions, *in this regard*.

I note these things and accept Hanan's point of view, that she represents some type of consensus. Her concern, which I share, is Palestinian rights *vis à vis* the Israelis and she rightly places them ahead of internal divisions. Her belief in the peace process as the best way out for the Palestinians stops her from entertaining doubts about the questionable nature of her mandate.

I decide to continue with questions about the Palestinian situation in general. 'What are you trying to achieve for the Palestinians? Is the emphasis on human rights or on land rights?'

'Human rights and land rights are indivisible. The body of international law governing belligerent occupations, the Hague Convention of 1907 and the Geneva Convention of 1949, clearly prohibit such acts as the establishment of Israeli settlements on occupied land and transfer the population of the occupier into occupied territory. Israeli violations of human and land rights violate international law, the will of the international community and the rights of the Palestinian people. They are also in defiance of the principles and requirements of the current peace process. Our vision of

Palestinian rights is integrated and interdependent. These rights must be exercised by our people on our own land, on Palestinian soil.'

Again, the answer appears conclusive, it has a finality which reflects the attitude of someone in a hurry, someone who is deeply concerned about Israeli land-grabs and how they are making life impossible for the Palestinians and forcing them to leave (since 1967, Israel has expropriated seventy-two per cent of the land of the occupied territories under one pretext or another). Not only is Ashrawi in the business of taking things back to basics, she genuinely fears that Israel's traditional resort to meaningless cosmetic measures – and I place most of Israeli Prime Minister Rabin's recent actions in this category – might cloud the issue and make it appear they're conceding in a meaningful way. In this regard, her answer to the Reuters' correspondent's question about an Israeli offer to allow the Palestinians to run their own hospitals met with a simple, 'but we've always done that.' (She's totally right; my thorough investigation of this area reveals that Israel has done nothing in the health care area since 1967, despite the clear responsibility it bears under international law and the Geneva Convention.)

At this point I decided that Hanan Ashrawi's knowledge of international law makes this well-covered area a futile one for further questioning. Believing as I do that the emergence of a Palestinian state is inevitable, I decided to concentrate on the more fundamental elements of what the Palestinians might get from one. 'What do you have to say about serious allegations of corruption among the rank and file of the PLO in Tunis?' When I tried to withdraw the question, Hanan gallantly told me that it is my right to ask any question and proceeded to answer it.

'I do not deal with rumour and innuendo. Wherever and whenever my problems exist, the proper path to a solution lies through democratic procedures, public accountability and continued vigilance and responsibility. The Palestinians, fortunately, have corrective mechanisms in their organizations and the democratic spirit to make them effective.'

With this straightforward answer, it was I who had a

serious decision to make. Hanan, consistently, places the Palestinian-Israeli problem before problems within the Palestinian community. Furthermore, she does believe in the Palestinians' ability to corect their mistakes. While I agree that the Israeli policy of creating facts by settling the occupied territories supersedes all else, I am also painfully aware of the level of corruption within the PLO and believe that Yasser Arafat is culpable and must do something about it immediately – before it affects his position of leadership and damages the Palestinian cause in the process. I accept her answer, not because I find it satisfactory, but because her occupation with what comes first is genuine, because I know she is whistle clean and because her commitment to the democratic process is a major subtle strike against inherent Arab corruption.

At this point, I decide that the time has come to concentrate on the problems of the Christians of the Holy Land. 'What about the Palestinian Christians? What future do you see for them under the present conditions?'

'The fate of the Christian community is indivisible from the destiny of the Palestinian people as a whole: occupation and exile certainly do not distinguish on the basis of religion. The attacks on the Al Aqsa Mosque and the seizure of St John's Hospice in Jerusalem are of equal concern to all Palestinians. Our present society and the future state we aim to build are founded on religious tolerance and freedom, as our declaration of independence clearly states. (The Palestinians declared a state four years ago, but for diplomatic reasons have not followed that with the formation of a government, though the PLO is essentially a Palestinian government in exile.) At present, the emigration of Palestinian Christians, caused by the harsh conditions of occupation, gives rise to concern that the community at the birthplace of Christianity is being depleted.'

This statement contains a stubborn refusal to deal with the Christians of the Holy land as a separate problem. Palestinianism is what is threatened, according to Hanan. A future for the Palestinians would entail, create, conditions which would ease the overall problem and cancel the

subsidiary one of the Christian community. But, aware as I
am that the pressure on the Christians comes from both sides,
the Israelis and the Muslim fundamentalists, the answer
leaves me unconvinced and somewhat worried. I make a last
attempt to isolate the problem of the Christians by asking
whether, in Hanạn's opinion, the churches in the West are
doing enough to help their co-religionists cope with the
overwhelming problems facing them.

'There is still much to be done and many challenges for the
churches, particularly those in the West, to face with
candour and courage. There have been times when churches
in the West, burdened by a heritage of guilt, have hesitated
to act when peace and justice demanded a greater commitment. Since at least 1982, however, there has been a marked
improvement. For a church to fulfil its mission, it must be
committed and active. The churches have a responsibility to
the Palestinian people as a whole, not just the Christian
community, and they must tackle the Palestinian problem in
its entirety. Of course the Palestinian Christian churches
need specific assistance and, most importantly, recognition –
the very churches which are bearers of Christian authenticity
have often been ignored and their voices have been silenced.
Sadly, a number of the evangelical denominations support
the State of Israel for fundamentalist reasons in direct
negation of Christian values and ethics. Our model should be
clergy like Bishop Desmond Tutu, who preached in the
Shepherds' Field in 1989 in a universal and loving spirit of
justice for all and against the oppression of the Palestinians
and all other peoples. The churches in the West also
urgently need to come to a greater understanding and
dialogue with Islam. Religion must connect humanity, not
build barriers.'

The answer is an admirable summation of all I had learned
in months of researching the problems of the Christians of
the Holy Land. But while all the problems, except for the
failure of the local churches to do their duty, are thoroughly
identified, they're still subordinated to the larger Palestinian
one.

'But what about Islamic fundamentalism? It is obvious

they have a measure of success in the occupied territories and that this creates a problem for the Christians.'

'Perhaps it is more to the point to say that there is a tide of religious fundamentalism all over the world, whether Islamic, Jewish or Christian. Islamic political groups in the occupied territories will become stronger, if the peace process doesn't offer concrete accomplishments and move us towards our goal of self-determination and statehood. Like any society, we will continue to have our opposition and other political voices. In Israel, however, fundamentalists are in power and translate their vision into racist policies.'

This is a good although incomplete answer. The existence of a worldwide resurgence of religious fundamentalism doesn't cancel its local importance and the desire to solve local problems. The nature and pressures of fundamentalist movements vary, and in many countries they are remote and isolated; they don't combine with other pressures to create intolerable situations and they are not strong enough to threaten a takeover. However, Hanan's point about Jewish fundamentalism being in power in Israel is valid and, judged by any yardstick, Israel is a theocratic state with all the intolerance that implies, and Israeli religious leaders openly ask for the expulsion of all Arabs from the occupied territories.

'But what about Islamic fundamentalist pamphlets distributed in the West Bank which attacked you personally and objected to your role in the peace negotiations?'

'Islamic political organizations have the rights to express themselves on issues, but I don't condone attacking individuals. A recent agreement between Fatah and Hammas (the largest Islamic fundamentalist group), concluded in late May, which includes a commitment to refrain from attacking individuals, offers a mechanism for serious and responsible debate on issues, rather than personalities. Even before this accord, I should note that I was never attacked as a Christian.

'Our situation under occupation, where open discussion and publication are often forbidden, places serious obstacles in the path of democratic exchange of views. Indeed, the occupation authorities foster division and stir up conflict, including forging leaflets and other practices. The authorities have waged a systematic campaign of disinformation against the Palestinian delegation, for example. Campaigns of disinformation have not attacked Christians, but political disagreements, in line with general policy.

The end of the interview found me going back to my original notion of seeing Hanan Ashrawi as two people, a Palestinian of solid credentials and a Christian of reluctant admission. Because her views represent those of many other Christians, this opens the door for me to extend my judgement to cover the many Christians who are determined to overlook their immediate problems or who see them as indivisible from the larger Palestinian one.

A minority, particularly a loyal one with no desire to separate itself from the whole surrounding it, cherishes a sense of belonging above all else. This can be a positive force when Christians like Hanan Ashrawi use it to work and contribute more than others, when they excel. But, and the answer is beyond the scope of this book, is it a positive force when the desire to belong is achieved at the expense of all else, when it translates into a blind attachment which ignores the obvious? Indeed, is it a positive force when members of that minority continue to behave in a diminished way which perpetuates their minority status?

Most Christians are afraid to state that their middle-class position renders them more vulnerable; even their obvious control of the tourist business causes them anxiety because admitting them might drive a wedge between them and their fellow Muslims. Most are certainly afraid to admit the problem caused by the rise of Islamic fundamentalism for the same reason. Many insist that their diminishing numbers is a Palestinian problem and not a Christian problem. And naturally, critcizing the PLO would make them more vulnerable because it would leave them without a political body to which they could attach themselves (the remaining choices of Israel and the fundamentalists are out of the question).

These fears are genuine; they force a pretence which stands in the way of separateness. But if this is acceptable from the ranks of average Christians then I would expect Christian political leadership to see beyond that and to behave in an unencumbered Palestinian way which is not so reduced and restricted as to render them incomplete – and stands in the way of telling the world of their plight. Like him or not, George Habbash has managed to transcend these fears and take a clear wholly Palestinian stand without suffering for it. And in the 1930s, Hannah Atallah, a Christian lawyer and businessman who was approached by my father to contribute to the nationalist cause, showed no reluctance to tell him off. Atallah resented being reminded of his duty and sent my father away after telling him that and asking him to tell the Mufti that members of his family had been pocketing his donations. By casting away all limitations and refusing to act in a frightened manner, they contributed to a wholesome picture of themselves as unapologetic Palestinians and were accepted, indeed honoured, as such.

This is why I cannot agree with Ashrawi and people who think like her. She is an outstanding spokesperson for the Palestinians in international forums, but if we are denied the benefit of her noble voice when the questions of bigotry and corruption are raised then she forfeits her position as a Palestinian leader and accepts considerably less than she and the Palestinians, Christian and Muslim alike, deserve.

AN UNCERTAIN FUTURE

That the Christians of the Holy Land are threatened with extinction cannot be denied. In a world which is witnessing the re-emergence of hitherto dormant religious and ethnic identities, this situation is extraordinary and demands attention.

But beyond the sympathy they undoutedly deserve, the situation of the Palestinian Christians has to be judged in terms of the power politics of the Middle East and the world in general. In this context the simple question of human sympathy becomes more complex and it is transformed into another one of whether the Palestinian Christians are worth saving and, if so, what should be done to help them. In the absence of a singular organization or governmental body that could provide a universally accepted answer, all the parties involved in deciding or influencing the fate of the Palestinian Christians must speak on an individual basis.

There is no doubt that the Christians of the Holy Land retain an identity of their own, not separate from the Palestinian one but distinguished by their social position within it. This identity has been moulded by many historical events not of the community's making, but this doesn't matter and in fact the Israeli policy of singling them out confirms their special identity and the tragedy attached to it. What is more important is that the Christian presence in the Holy Land reaches far back into history, so much so that it is amusing to hear some Palestinian Christians refer to settlers at the time of the Crusades as newcomers.

I have not interviewed, heard of or read about a single Christian layman, political or business leader or religious personality who doesn't express an attractive commitment to their Christian and Palestinian identity. Even Palestinians who appear to concentrate on criticizing their Muslim compatriots, like Roman Catholic patriarch Michel Sabbah, exhibit genuine pain at the thought of the diminished status and presence of their co-religionists. And while it is human, and totally natural, for many Christians to respond to the pressures surrounding them by emigrating, many soldier on against all odds, and they exhibit an enviable Christian spirit which supports the oft-made claim that Holy Land Christianity, through suffering, will teach wider Christianity and the rest of the world something of value.

Sadly, this community spirit is not matched by an equal commitment on the part of the local churches, even when some of the leaders of these churches profess otherwise. The local churches do not reflect the courage and steadfastness of their followers, and most of the time they do not even reflect their followers' opinions. The local churches are hampered by old ideas which vitiate their effectiveness when it is most needed, and they are tied to the idea of saving people's souls in an atmosphere which cries for help in improving their daily life.

But to judge the Christians of the Holy Land by the antiquated ideas of their churches is to accept the churches' defenition of what is at stake. Any true judgement of the Palestinian Christian condition must begin and end with the people, particularly in view of the fact that the people have a difficult time accepting their churches and the churches have not suffered. (The lifestyle of many church leaders is highly questionable, if not altogether unacceptable.)

The Christians of the Holy Land, all of them from the shopkeeper to the political leader, want to continue where they are. Their claim is historic and their achievements and contributions to the Palestinian community as a whole are clear. They have reason to believe that they are worth saving, and cannot comprehend how others see a threat in their innocent presence. All one has to do is see them close to the land or at prayer in the churches of the Holy Sepulchre or of the Nativity to be touched by their close relationship to where they are. And if one listens to those who have emigrated to the United States, Latin America, Canada or Australia one is struck by their spiritual attachment to the Holy Land. In terms of everyday happenings the Christian presence in the Holy Land is in the contributions of Hanan Ashrawi, Jad Izhaq, Anton Sansour and the likes of Camille Nassar and Doris Salah.

But, beyond the Christian community itself, how do the Palesteinians in general view the prospect of Christian disappearance? How do Palestinian Muslims feel about it? Because of the traditional Arab way of pretending things aren't what they are, this is probably the most difficult question on their future to get answered. Beyond sugar-coating the unacceptable, there is a considerable difference between what people say and what they do.

There is an implicit and explicit attempt to deny the existence of a 'Christian problem'. This denial is practised by Christians and Muslims alike. On both sides, most people either relegate the problem to a secondary position, behind that of the Israeli occupation, or dismiss it as transitory and insignificant. This is dishonest, and harmful, a mere wish to concentrate on the common enemy, Israel. It is a wish to maintain Palestinian solidarity, or a reflection of the fear that talking about it will make things worse – or a hope that it will disappear.

The reality which is often denied but must be confronted is different. Islamic fundamentalism, the Hammas, Islamic Jihad and Army of Mohammad movements, are gaining strength to such an extent that it is easy to observe them without reference to the well-meant denials. They recently won the muncipal elections in the town of Ramallah in the face of opposition from a Christian-Muslim coalition (remarkable when one takes into consideration that the Christians represent a quarter of the population). Estimates of Islamic fundamentalist strength vary, but on a conservative reckoning it probably amounts to at least twenty-five per cent of the vote of the occupied territories.

The Islamic fundamentalist movement is blind and intolerant, an expression of the politics of vengeance against a perfidious West, an extension of the Crusades. It accuses the local Christians of being a fifth column, of being beholden to Christian influences, which are anti-Muslim, anti-Arab, and anti-Palestinian. The fact that the history of the local Christians and their every day activities negate this accusation does not register with Muslim religious zealots and all attempts to convert them to a more reasonable attitude are doomed to failure.

Luckily, without attempting to downplay the Muslim fundamentalist threat, the PLO, with all its faults, is still the leading political movement in the occupied territories. The PLO isn't only secular, its leadership recognizes the value of its Christian constituency. Not only are Christians accepted without discrimination in its ranks, but Yasser Arafat himself is married to a Christian and his refusal to require his wife to convert to Islam is a measure of his lack of discrimination and an inherent decency which is often clouded by the unacceptable acts of his subordinates.

With this as background it is safe to assume a Palestinian decision in favour of unhamperd Christian existence, so long as this is a PLO decision. But were the raging struggle between the PLO and Muslim fundamentalists to tilt in favour of the latter, then the Christians of the Holy Land would become more vulnerable than ever and the emerging constraints on their way of life and isolated anti-Christian incidents would increase. However one feels about the PLO, their position regarding the Christians is to be commended.

But, as in many other instances and places, it is the people outside politics who have the last word on how things should be; and there are thousands of Palestinians who fall into this category. This is why my cousin Khalil's statement about the Christian contribution to things Palestinian is important and why so many others like him subscribe to the same healthy view.

Beyond the Palestinian attitude towards their own

Christians is the more intractable view of other Arabs. With the exception of Iraq, most of the Arab countries level the same accusations of dual loyalty at the fourteen million Arab Christians. Coupled with a rise in Islamic fundamentalism, this attitude has made Christian life very difficult. For the most part, the Arab countries see the Christians as representatives of a problem which they would prefer to ignore.

This marginalization takes the form of insensitivity to their problems. The unwholesome role being played in the occupied territories by Saudi Arabia represents a stark example of this lack of care. Determined to undermine the leadership of Yasser Arafat with whom it is conducting a political feud, Saudi Arabia has provided the Islamic fundamentalist movement of the occupied territories with funds. In origin, this policy is not aimed at the Christians, but it produces anti-Christian results. This example of short-sighted meddling should be condemned outright.

The attitude of benign neglect adopted by Arab countries has profound psychological effects. The widespread refusal to accept George Habbash because of his terrorist background while hosting the clearly terroristic Abu Nidal is resented by all Christians, even those who decidedly oppose Habbash's ways. And the refusal to channel funds to the occupied territories through well-qualified Christian charity organizations and the choice of less qualified Muslim ones, is dispiriting, especially when one is dealing with institutions such as hospitals.

Put simply, the Arab governments would like to see the Palestinian Christians disappear. This wish may not assume the form of overt action, but it does contribute to an overall Christian estrangement from the Middle East body politic. Even Christian thinkers and educators are not accorded the importance they deserve. Islamic militancy has infected the attitude of most Middle East governments, including the ones threatened by it – they find it easier to accommodate rather than confront the movement.

How the Palestinian Christians feel about the mainline churches in the West has been thoroughly detailed and demonstrated, but getting the churches in the West to adopt an understandable open position regarding the Palestinian Christians is more difficult. The statements on the subject one gets from Rome or Canterbury are examples of meaningless diplomatic jargon, and the Greek Orthodox Church declines to make any comment at all.

Judged by their actions, these churches are only providing weak support, substantially less than required and often misdirected. It isn't only that the churches have problems closer to home and bigger ones in other parts of the world; there is the further element of being afraid of Palestinian Christianity. The mainline churches cringe at the prospect of being led into uncharted territory by people they see as politically unreliable, people very different from their docile and desensitized Western parishioners.

Hard as it my sound, and with consideration for the diversity of attitude, one is forced to conclude that the mainline Christian churches are not averse to seeing the Palestinian Christians leave the Holy Land and absolve them of their brotherly and moral obligations. They have no problem accepting a Holy Land Christian presence based on politically neutral church representation and ownership of land. In fairness, people like the Quakers and Lutherans see the situation of the Palestinian Christians for the human tragedy it is and try to help. The guilty parties are the churches with local parishioners, the Catholics, Greek Orthodox and Anglicans who view their obligations with something resembling a malevolent detachment.

This is the most shameful betrayal of them all. It goes beyond an evasion of moral duty, it contains disturbing racial implications which fly in the face of Christian teachings. It may very well represent a worldwide church attitude; in either case it deserves unqualified condemnation.

The rest of the world has no idea how to handle the problem of the Palestinian Christians. Because they have refused to separate themselves from their Muslim compatriots, they cannot be identified as a distinct ethnic group, as indeed they are not, and distinguishing them on the basis of religious affiliation might prove counterproductive. They are not Kurds, Armenians or Yugoslav Muslims and their

Palestinianism and Christianity appear to adhere together in inseparable union.

So the world sees them as Palestinians, with minor modifications, and it relegates them to a component in a wider picture with which it has failed to deal. But it goes beyond that, and there is implicit scorn of the Palestinian Christians; the world doesn't really understand why they would want to remain loyal to a national identity which denies them sympathy and deters others from helping them.

So the verdict on the Palestinian Christians isn't unanimous. Only they themselves and most of their Muslim compatriots think Palestinian Christianity is worth saving. The rest – and Israel's antipathy towards them is taken for granted – the mainline churches, the Arabs and most of the rest of the world, have no interest in their fate. Yet, because we are in an age which purports to support people's rights to self-determination, it is the Palestinian Christians' perception of themselves and their future which matters. The Christians want to stay in the Holy Land, and therefore they deserve to be saved.

Here it is well to remember again that we are talking about a community with deep historical roots. We're also talking about one of the most educated communities in the Third World, and that Palestinian Christians' contributions in the fields of politics, education and the arts have had a salutary effct on the rest of the Middle East. Furthermore, a healthy Christian presence in the Holy Land may provide a needed voice of moderation between a militant Islam and Israeli brutality.

Amazingly the complexity of the problem of the Holy Land Christians does not reduce the number of ways available to help them and there are things that could and should be done to reduce the pressures forcing them to leave. However, coordinating action by the parties capable of helping is impossible, and I am forced to deal with them on an individual basis.

Undoubtedly the mainline churches are the bodies which could do most to help the Christians of the Holy Land. They're already there; they have a presence; and their relationship with the local Christian community may be strained, but it is established. Also, they have room to do a lot because they have done so little.

Above all the mainline churches are under an obligation to provide the Christians of the Holy Land with moral and psychological support by coming clean on where they stand *vis-à-vis* their problem with Israel. The present ambiguous diplomatic line they follow must come to an end; it has done nothing except prolong the agony of the local Christians and erode their faith in the mother churches.

Beyond this important initial step, a concrete change in the nature of the aid provided by the churches is necessary. Charity is, by definition, a stop-gap measure. It should give way to structural aid programmes aimed at utilizing the available talent of the Christians. Small industry could be developed, aided by a church commitment to buy certain products from the Holy Land. And the churches could do considerably more to encourage tourism to the Holy Land.

The world community is under an obligation to speak out on some issues and stop lumping all the Palestinian together as an excuse – as if it were. The Israelis' attempts to wrest the tourist business from the hands of the Christians and the methods used to do so are a good starting point. This is a clear problem of human rights and must be recognized as such. The US, UK, France and Germany and other governments are fully capable of attaching strings to their aid and cooperation programmes with Israel until and unless this discriminatory policy is changed. Identifying this problem as a humanitarian rather than a political issue would make this action possible without causing too much fuss. Lastly, these governments are also capable of providing encouragement to small industries, either directly or by prompting national corporations to participate in such an effort.

The Arab countries, corrupt and insensitive as they are, must take the situation of the Palestinian Christians into account. Specifically, aid to the occupied territories must not be made on a religious basis to the exclusion of the Christians and their effective organizations. Both the YMCA and YWCA are shining examples of active non-discrimination and should be helped, and Christian institutions of higher education and vocational training centres must be supported. And blind harmful politics such as Saudi support for the local Islamic fundamentalist movement must be ended. I find it utterly appalling that President Bush and Prime Minister Major see fit to heap praise on a regressive Saudi regime at a time when its actions are threatening Christian life in the Holy Land. The Palestinians themselves should do more to stem the flow of talent out of the Holy Land. A first step would be for the PLO to recognize the individuality of the Christian problem without indulging in divisive politics. Yasser Arafat would do well to divert some of the money he spends in the occupied territories on corrupt political cronies into constructive down-to-earth efforts similar to those being made by many Christian organizations. And he should encourage a wider Muslim–Christian dialogue than already exists.

The local churches, like the mother churches, must come clean on some issues. They must put their obligation to the local community before their adherence to other political objectives of the mother churches. The latter espouse impractical policies unrelated to local conditions. The churches, particularly the Greek Orthodox and Roman Catholic ones, must cease to see themselves simply as custodians of a questionable historical presence and involve themselves more directly in social work. Above all, the local churches should stop their bickering and backbiting and cooperate towards a common good.

I have no message for the Israelis or the Muslim fundamentalists. Israel is a religious state which has a great deal in common with Islamic fundamentalism; both advocate the creation of theocracies. It is for the world to see the Israeli government and Islamic fundamentalist movement for what they are. It is for people of goodwill everywhere to deny them the aid and comfort which allow them to practise their policies.

The Christians of the Holy Land continue to behave with honour. My heart and mind ache for them. Honour to them, now and always, and may their wish to teach the Arabs, Christians and the rest of the world a lesson in forbearance come true.